Leckie×Leckie
Scotland's leading educational publishers

£6.99

Practice Papers for SQA Exams

Higher

History

Text © John A. Kerr
Design and layout © 2011 Leckie & Leckie

01/080411

Questions and answers do not emanate from SQA. All of our entirely new and original Practice Papers have been written by experienced authors working directly for the publisher.

ISBN 978-1-84372-796-5

Published by
Leckie & Leckie Ltd
An imprint of HarperCollins*Publishers*
Westerhill Road, Bishopbriggs, Glasgow, G64 2QT
T: 0844 576 8126   F: 0844 576 8131
leckieandleckie@harpercollins.co.uk   www.leckieandleckie.co.uk

Special thanks to
Helen Bleck (proofreader)
Exemplarr (creative packaging)
Roda Morrison (copy-editor)
Jennifer Richards (proofreader)

A CIP Catalogue record for this book is available from the British Library.

Acknowledgements
Leckie & Leckie has made every effort to trace all copyright holders.
If any have been inadvertently overlooked, we will be pleased to make the necessary arrangements.

We would like to thank the following for permission to reproduce their material:
Hodder Education for two extracts from *The Scottish Wars of Independence 1286-1328* by Andy MacPhee [2010] (Source A on page 21 and Source B on page 33) and for an extract from *Scotland and the Impact of the Great War 1914-1928* by John A. Kerr [2010] (Source E on page 27), all reproduced by permission of Hodder Education.
The Saltire Society for an extract from *The Union of Scotland and England* by P. H. Scott (Source A on page 24) and an extract from *Scotland's Relations with England* by William Ferguson (Source E on page 25).
Herald & Times Group for an extract from the *Glasgow Herald*, issue dated 14 April 1923 (Source C on page 27).
Janet Stenhouse for an extract from a lecture (Source C on page 33).
Peter Newark's Pictures for reproduction of a poster (Source A on page 35).
Dumfries and Galloway Council. Licensor www.scran.ac.uk for reproduction of a poster (Source A on page 38).
Birlinn Ltd for an extract from *Voices from War* by Ian MacDougall (Source B on page 38).

Further copyright acknowledgements may be found by going to http://www.leckieandleckie.co.uk
and navigating to the Higher History Practice Papers page.

32302941176
donation
(907.6)

Mixed Sources
Product group from well-managed
forests and other controlled sources
www.fsc.org Cert no. SW-COC-001806
© 1996 Forest Stewardship Council

FSC is a non-profit international organisation
established to promote the responsible management
of the world's forests. Products carrying the FSC
label are independently certified to assure consumers
that they come from forests that are managed to
meet the social, economic and ecological needs
of present and future generations.

Find out more about HarperCollins
and the environment at
www.harpercollins.co.uk/green

Introduction

Layout of the book

This book contains advice, practice exam questions and marking instructions which will help you prepare for the SQA examination in Higher History.

The layout, paper colour and types of question are all similar to the actual exam you will sit, so that you become familiar with what the exam paper will look like.

This book also contains marking advice and outline answers for all the questions. These marking schemes are at the back of the book and they all follow a standard pattern, similar in some ways to the marking instructions given to markers by the SQA.

The exam papers in this book are specially written to show you what you can expect in the Higher History exam from 2011 onwards.

What is in this book?

As there is a huge choice of topics in Higher History this set of practice papers does not cover every topic. Instead, the papers here cover the most popular topics.

In Paper 1 the topics examined are:

- Britain 1851–1951
- Germany 1815–1939
- The USA 1918–1968
- Appeasement and the Road to War, to 1939

In Paper 2, four of the possible five topics on Scottish history are examined.

These topics are:

- The Wars of Independence, 1286–1328
- The Treaty of Union, 1689–1740
- Migration and Empire, 1830–1939
- Scotland and the Impact of the Great War, 1914–1928

How are the exam papers arranged?

You will find two sets of exam papers in this book. They are called Higher History Examination A and Higher History Examination B.

For Paper 1, Examination Paper A and Examination Paper B have full sets of essay questions for all four topics covered.

For Paper 2, Examination Paper A and Examination Paper B have full sets of source-based questions for each of the topics detailed below.

Examination Paper A has full sets of questions on the following Scottish history topics:

- The Wars of Independence, 1286–1328
- The Treaty of Union, 1689–1740
- Scotland and the Impact of the Great War, 1914–1928

Examination Paper B has full sets of questions on the following Scottish history topics:

- The Wars of Independence, 1286–1328
- Migration and Empire, 1830–1939
- Scotland and the Impact of the Great War, 1914–1928

Warning!

In 2011 the Higher History exam changed so beware of using exam papers from earlier years to practise. They will not reflect the exam you will sit!

How to use this book

The Topic Index allows you to find all the questions within the book that deal with a specific topic or a specific question type. This allows you to focus on areas that you particularly want to revise or – if you are only part way through your course – it allows you to practise answering exam-style questions for just those topics that you have studied so far.

The next section is called Exam Skills. You can use this section to develop your skills on exam technique by looking at the specific types of question and how best to answer them. (Exam technique really just means the ways in which you can answer the questions efficiently and effectively.)

Higher History Paper 1 is entirely based on essay-type questions. There is specific advice in this book on how to write effective, high-scoring essays. There are also tips on how to take short cuts to getting good marks!

In Higher History Paper 2 you answer four source-based questions on **one** of the study topics only. Each of the four types of question is different but this book provides a step-by-step guide to what you need to do to score well.

This book allows you to complete an entire practice paper as preparation for the final exam if you wish. You can complete the exam paper under exam-style conditions by setting yourself a time for each paper and answering it as well as possible without using any references or notes, or alternatively you can answer part of the exam paper as a revision exercise using the marking schemes provided here to produce a good, well-structured answer. Your teacher may mark your answers and provide feedback.

Finally, at the back of the book, you will find marking advice on how to answer the questions along with top exam tips.

Topic Index – Paper 1

Topic	Exam A, Paper 1	Exam B, Paper 1	Knowledge for Prelim			Knowledge for SQA Exam		
			Have difficulty	Still needs work	OK	Have difficulty	Still needs work	OK
Later Modern History: Britiain 1851-1951								
• Issue 1. An evaluation of the reasons why Britain became more democratic, 1851-1928.	1							
• Issue 2. An assessment of how democratic Britain became, 1867-1928.		1						✓
• Issue 3. An evaluation of the reasons why women won greater political equality by 1928.	2							
• Issue 4. An evaluation of the reasons why the Liberals introduced social welfare reforms, 1906-1914.		2						
• Issue 5. An assessment of the effectiveness of the Liberal social welfare reforms.	3							
• Issue 6. An assessment of the effectiveness of the Labour social welfare reforms, 1945-1951.		3						
Later Modern History: Germany 1815-1939								
• Issue 1. An evaluation of the reasons for the growth of nationalism in Germany, 1815-1850.	4							
• Issue 2. An assessment of the degree of growth of nationalism in Germany, up to 1850.		4						
• Issue 3. An evaluation of the obstacles to German unification, 1815-1850.	5							
• Issue 4. An evaluation of the reasons why unification was achieved in Germany, by 1871.		5						
• Issue 5. An evaluation of the reasons why the Nazis achieved power in 1933.	6							
• Issue 6. An evaluation of the reasons why the Nazis were able to stay in power, 1933-1939.		6						
Later Modern History: USA 1918-68								
• Issue 1. An evaluation of the reasons for changing attitudes towards immigration in the 1920s.	7							
• Issue 2. An evaluation of the obstacles to the achievement of civil rights for black people up to 1941.		7						
• Issue 3. An evaluation of the reasons for the economic crisis of 1929-33.	8							
• Issue 4. An assessment of the effectiveness of the New Deal.		8						
• Issue 5. An evaluation of the reasons for the development of the Civil Rights campaign, after 1945.	9							
• Issue 6. An assessment of the effectiveness of the Civil Rights movement in meeting the needs of black Americans, up to 1968.		9						
Later Modern History: Appeasement and the Road to War, to 1939								
• Issue 1. An evaluation of the reasons for the aggressive nature of the foreign policies of Germany and Italy in the 1930s.	10							
• Issue 2. An assessment of the methods used by Germany and Italy to pursue their foreign policies from 1933.		10						
• Issue 3. An evaluation of the reasons for the British policy of appeasement, 1936-1938.	11							
• Issue 4. An assessment of the success of British foreign policy in containing fascist aggression, 1935-March 1938.		11						
• Issue 5. An assessment of the Munich agreement.	12							
• Issue 6. An evaluation of the reasons for the decision to abandon the policy of appeasement and for the outbreak of war in 1939.		12						

Topic Index – Paper 2

Topic	Exam A, Paper 2	Exam B, Paper 2	Knowledge for Prelim			Knowledge for SQA Exam		
			Have difficulty	Still needs work	OK	Have difficulty	Still needs work	OK
The Wars of Independence, 1286-1328								
• Issue 1. Scotland 1286-96: the succession problem and the Great Cause.	1	1						
• Issue 2. John Balliol and Edward I.	2	2						
• Issue 3. William Wallace and Scottish resistance.	3	3						
• Issue 4. The rise and triumph of Robert Bruce.	4	4						
The Treaty of Union, 1689-1740								
• Issue 1. Worsening relations with England.	1							
• Issue 2. Arguments for and against union with England.	2							
• Issue 3. The passing of the Act of Union.	3							
• Issue 4. The effects of the Union, to 1740.	4							
Migration and Empire, 1830-1939								
• Issue 1. The migration of Scots.		1						
• Issue 2. The experience of immigrants in Scotland.		2						
• Issue 3. The impact of Scots emigrants on the Empire.		3						
• Issue 4. The effects of migration and empire on Scotland, to 1939.		4						
Scotland and the Impact of the Great War, 1914-1928								
• Issue 1. Scots on the Western Front.	1	1						
• Issue 2. Domestic impact of war: society and culture.	2	2						
• Issue 3. Domestic impact of war: industry and economy.	3	3						
• Issue 4. Domestic impact of war: politics.	4	4						

Exam Skills

Preparing for the exam

Long before you sit the exam you must be clear about exactly what you have to do in the exam room. Do not assume that any NAB assessment that you will sit in class time will be the same as the exam. It will **not** be the same. The NAB may be identical to a part of the exam but no NAB covers the full content or the full time allowed for the exam.

Higher History Paper 1

The Paper 1 examination has a time allocation of 1 hour 20 minutes.

Your target is to write **two** essays in those 80 minutes. Remember that is one essay from the British History Historical Study and one from the European/World Historical Study.

All questions in Paper 1 require you to write a properly constructed essay in answer to the question.

What should you do first when you open your exam question booklet?

- Make yourself think. Breathe deeply. You will be nervous and adrenaline will be pumping. You will want to get started quickly, but take your time.

- Make sure you are looking at the questions in the section of the course you have actually studied.

- Look for questions you might want to answer.

- Make sure you have understood not only what the question is about but also what you have to do. In other words, see what the topic is but also what the task is.

- Finally, read all the questions again in your chosen topic and make sure the one you have chosen gives you the best chance to score highly.

The single most important piece of advice to any candidate is **read the question and decide what it is asking you to do**.

The SQA has reported that if candidates would only read each question carefully and work out what it asks them to do, it would make a massive contribution to raising standards of performance. Every year markers find a significant number of essays written by candidates who seem to have prepared answers before the exam and use these regardless of the exact wording of the actual exam questions. Don't be one of these candidates. In other words, you must pay attention to **topic** and **task**.

TOP EXAM TIP

The first things you should look for in any essay question are **topic** and **task**. The topic is what event or person or time period is asked about in the question. The task is what you have to **do** with your information on the subject. You will always have to make some sort of decision or judgement about the topic.

You score K marks for including accurate and relevant information about the topic but it is answering the task that gets A marks. (See next page.)

How to write a good essay

Although each essay will have a different title and be on a different topic, **all** essays must have the same basic layout and all will be marked in the same way.

Your essay will be marked in three separate sections.

- There is a maximum of 4 marks for **structure** (called S marks).
- There is a maximum of 6 marks for **factual knowledge** (called K marks).
- There is a maximum of 10 marks for **analysis** (called A marks).

Structure (S marks)

To gain good marks for **structure** your essay must have:

- an introduction;
- good development of your answer;
- a conclusion.

The **introduction** is the most vital part of any essay.

It should provide a clear indication of the route you intend to take through your essay and introduce the points which will be developed throughout the rest of it.

A good introduction should set the essay title in its context, indicate the relevant factors you will develop throughout your essay and also sketch out the main arguments you will use to answer the question.

As you write your essay you should be able to refer back to your introduction as a guide to remind you what each paragraph should be about.

> **TOP EXAM TIP**
>
> Plan to include in your introduction **only** the main points that you will develop in your essay. Do not explain any points in your introduction. There are no K marks for information included in your introduction.
>
> Be realistic. There is no point in including so many points in your introduction that you have no time to develop them all. As part of your revision you should plan out the critical points you need to include in an introduction.

Every introduction should start by setting the **context**. The context should take no more than two or three sentences. Context just means the background information that sets the scene for the answer.

You will see in every essay marking scheme that there is a context written for you. It is there just to show you how long the context part of your answer should be and how much information should be in it.

> **TOP EXAM TIP**
>
> You could write and learn a context for every topic you prepare for the exam. A context does not help to answer the question, it merely sets the scene for the essay. With contexts, 'one size fits all' because a context for a topic will fit in with any question on that topic.

Look at this example of a good introduction to the question:

> To what extent did the Liberals hope to win political advantage by starting a programme of social reforms after 1906?

By the early 20th century, most men, rich and poor, could vote and the Liberals were worried about losing votes to the new Labour Party that emerged in 1900 and promised to campaign for social reform. [This sentence sets the context.] *Social reform could therefore be seen as a way to gain political advantage (1) but other factors played a part.*

The reforms were also the result of concern about poverty (2), highlighted in the reports of Booth and Rowntree. The spread of municipal socialism (3) inspired some Liberals to attempt social reform on a national scale. The Liberals were also concerned about Britain's declining national efficiency (4) and security (5). Finally, new attitudes in the Liberal Party, called New Liberalism (6), caused the Liberals to move away from the laissez-faire ideology of the 19th century.

TOP EXAM TIP

You will see there are six numbered marks in the above essay introduction. It is entirely up to you, but some students find it useful to number their main ideas with a pencil. The numbers help to show how many separate middle section paragraphs there should be to develop. They also provide a guide to what comes next once you start writing the essay. When you have written your essay **rub out the numbers!** In high quality essays numbers don't look very good!

Why is this a good introduction?

It is good because it sets the context, it makes it clear there were six main reasons for social reform that will be developed later and it outlines the argument that the Liberal reforms were the result of several pressures and were not based entirely on the hope of gaining political advantage.

The second main part of your structure is the **development section**.

This is quite an easy part of the process. All you have to do is make sure that the development part of your essay has:

- a separate paragraph for each main point that you numbered in your introduction;
- accurate and relevant information;
- a first sentence for each paragraph that makes clear what the point of the paragraph will be;
- clear links that make the paragraphs relevant to the overall title.

After one well-structured paragraph, go on to the next. This should be based on the next point raised in your introduction. It should follow the same advice, continuing your main argument and showing off more of your factual knowledge.

Here is a good development paragraph based on this question from the USA 1918–1968 topic:

How far was effective use of the media important to the success of the civil rights movement in the USA in the 1950s and 1960s?

The paragraph here develops the point that the winning of publicity gained public sympathy and was very important to the achievement of civil rights.

The gaining of sympathy and publicity by protests was a vital part of the success of the civil rights campaigns. When Rosa Parks refused to give up her seat on a bus in Montgomery, Alabama, she triggered a bus boycott which gained wide publicity and led to the emergence of an important civil rights leader, Martin Luther King – two vital ingredients in explaining why the campaigns were successful. Later, TV news film of the violent reaction of racist authorities during the protests in Birmingham, Alabama and on the Selma to Montgomery march gained widespread national and federal sympathy and support for the protestors.

The **conclusion** provides the third and final part of your structure mark.

Your essay **must** have a conclusion. The SQA says that to gain top marks, your conclusion:

- must be balanced;
- must summarise your arguments;
- must come to an overall judgement directly related to the question.

Here is an effective way to write a good conclusion.

Start by writing *In conclusion ...* and write one sentence that makes a general answer to the main question.

Then write *On one hand ...* and summarise the information that supports one point of view about the essay title.

Then write *On the other hand ...* and sum up the evidence that gives a different point of view about the main question.

Finally, write *Overall ...* and then write an overall answer to the main question, perhaps including what you think is the most important point made which led you to your final summary.

Here is an example of how to follow that pattern based on the question:

> How far did Britain become more of a democracy between 1867 and 1918?

In conclusion, Britain did become more democratic between 1867 and 1918 but was not yet fully a democracy. On one hand more people gained the right to vote, the system became fairer, there was more choice and people had access to information to make informed choices. On the other hand, women did not yet have full political equality with men. Overall, Britain was much more democratic than it had been in 1867 but still had some way to go, including reforming the UK 'first past the post' voting system which some people argue is still not democratic.

Knowledge (K marks)

The second set of marks you get are awarded for including accurate and relevant knowledge in your essay. You will get up to 6 marks for accurate and relevant factual knowledge. You will score 1 mark each time you use a correct piece of information to support a main point. You will get a second mark if you develop that information point further.

However, you will not get a mark for every piece of information you include. You will not get any K marks for knowledge given within your introduction, so keep to the point.

Supposing the question asked:

> How important was Bismarck to the unification of Germany?

Here is part of an answer to that question:

Bismarck fought three wars. The second was against Austria. He had settled the war with Denmark at the Convention of Gastein but this left Austria in a tricky position. When an argument broke out over the ruling of Holstein, Bismarck used it as an excuse to provoke a war with Austria. After a short seven-week war Austria was defeated at the Battle of Königgratz (also known as Sadowa). Prussian military tactics and technology were better and Prussian troops used the latest breech-loading needle gun. Austrian casualties were high. Bismarck then arranged a quick peace settlement with Austria at the Treaty of Prague....

And so on and so on.

In terms of knowledge there are at least ten hard facts in this answer. However, the detailed information just develops the one main point: that Bismarck used wars to assist his unification of Germany.

It would not be fair to give 6 out of 6 knowledge marks when there are so many other factors in German unification that have to be explained. So no matter how much factual information you write on one **part** of your answer, you will only score at most 2 marks for knowledge in each part.

Analysis or Argument (A marks)

You will get up to 10 marks (half your total for the entire essay) for using your information to answer the question asked. You must show you have understood the question and are using your information and ideas to answer the question directly. It is never enough just to tell a story!

Here is what the SQA says about the marks that can be given for analysis:

- If your essay is almost entirely storytelling (narrative) with little or no clear attempt to answer the question, you will get between 0 and 1 mark.

- If your essay is **mainly** narrative, but with brief attempts to answer the question, you will get between 2 and 3 marks.

- If your essay has some evidence used directly to answer the question but also still has some narrative sections you will get between 4 and 5 marks.

- If your evidence is used to support an argument that is directly focused on the question you will get between 6 and 7 marks.

- If there is sustained analysis with no drifting into narrative for its own sake you will get between 8 and 10 marks. For the top mark you should also have a balanced argument showing some awareness of different historical points of view. That does **not** mean you must include historians' names and quotes. There is nothing wrong with including them but they are not obligatory for high or even full marks.

One way to help make sure you are including analysis in your essay is to use the word **because**!

When you use some factual information make sure you link it to the question. For example, if you are asked how important fear of war was in the attempts to appease Hitler in 1938, you could write:

Many people had seen newsreels of the bombing of Guernica in the Spanish Civil War and were afraid that 'the bomber would always get through'. This was important in building up support for the policy of appeasement because ...

So, to summarise Paper 1:

Each essay you write in the exam is worth 20 marks.

The marking for each essay is divided up into:

- 4 marks for structure. Structure is divided into introduction, development and conclusion.

- 6 marks for knowledge. Knowledge must be relevant and accurate.

- 10 marks for analysis. It must be clear that the information in the essay is used to make a point that is relevant to answering the question.

Higher History Paper 2

From 2011 onwards, Paper 2 of your Higher History will be completely different from any earlier Higher History exam paper. Beware of using earlier past papers. They will not show what you have to do now.

The Paper 2 examination lasts for 1 hour 25 minutes.

Paper 2 will contain five different sets of sources and questions, one set for each special topic. You will only answer questions on **one** special topic. Each topic will have four questions.

Two of these questions will be worth 5 marks, two will be worth 10 marks.

In total, Paper 2 is worth 30 marks.

You should aim to **write** your 5-mark answers in around 10–12 minutes.
You should aim to **write** your 10-mark answers in about 20–25 minutes.
That will leave about 25 minutes for reading and thinking.

Remember, you need to read all the sources for the special topic on which you are answering the questions carefully, several times, think carefully and plan your answers. So do **not** spend longer writing your answers than the times shown above on each question.

> **TOP EXAM TIP**
>
> Make sure you practise answering questions in the time available to you in the exam. There is no point training for the exam by taking a long time over each answer. Make sure you have a watch. Not every exam room has a clock and timing is **vital**!

There are five Scottish-based special topics. These topics are:

- The Wars of Independence, 1286–1328
- The Age of the Reformation, 1542–1603
- The Treaty of Union, 1689–1740
- Migration and Empire, 1830–1939
- Scotland and the Impact of the Great War, 1914–1928

Remember: you answer questions on only **one** special topic!

One of the 5-mark questions will be a source evaluation question, also known as the 'How useful?' question. This will usually be identified by a question asking, 'How useful is Source ... as evidence of ...?' In this type of question you are being asked to judge how good the source is as a piece of historical evidence.

The other 5-mark question will be a comparison question. You will be asked to compare two points of view overall and in detail. The question **might not** use the word 'compare'. The wording of the question could be something like 'To what extent does Source B agree with Source C about ...?'

Two of the questions will be worth 10 marks. One will ask 'How fully?' This question is to test your knowledge of a whole issue.

The other 10-mark question will be a 'How far?' question. Remember, there are four issues in the syllabus that you can be examined on. The 'How far?' question is to test your knowledge on one specific part of an issue, called a sub issue. You can find all the sub issues in the column called 'detailed descriptors' on the SQA syllabus website at http://www.sqa.org.uk/files_ccc/History_Higher_2010.pdf

---

TOP EXAM TIP

In Paper 2, you need to know **all** about the topic you are studying. A 'How far' question can ask about **any** part of the detailed descriptors or **any** of the four main issues.

How to answer the 'How useful?' question

The source evaluation question is worth 5 marks. First, you must comment on **origin** and **purpose**. You will get **up to** 2 marks for writing about the source's origin (who wrote it or where the source first appeared) and its purpose (why the source was produced). To get the full 2 marks you must explain how that information makes the source useful in terms of the question.

Secondly, you must use **information from the source**. You will get **up to** 2 marks for explaining why the parts of the source you have selected are useful in terms of the question.

Thirdly, you must use **your own knowledge**. You will get **up to** 2 marks for using your own detailed knowledge as long as it is relevant to the question. This is called using relevant recall.

Finally, it is helpful to **make sure you have actually evaluated the source!**

For examples of answers to 'How useful?' questions see pages 61, 64, 67, 85, 89 and 93.

How to answer the comparison question

First, you must make **an overall comparison**. You will get up to 2 marks for stating and explaining the main ideas or opinions or points of view in the two sources. Secondly, you must compare them **in detail**. There are up to 4 marks available for this part of your answer. There will be four direct, relevant and fairly obvious comparison points for you to find.

You **must** show that you understand the points made in the sources and explain in what ways they differ from each other or support each other.

It is **not enough** just to list points of difference between the sources. In fact, you might get **no marks** for simply stating 'Source A says ... but B says ...'

However, you **will** get marks for making clear what the comparison connection is between the sources (possibly by quoting from each source). **You must also** explain in your own words the comparison points being made between the sources and, if it is relevant, you could bring in your own knowledge to further explain the comparison points.

For examples of answers to comparison questions see pages 61, 63, 68, 87, 91 and 95.

How to answer the 'How far?' question

Remember, there are four issues within each special study topic. Each issue is divided into separate parts called 'descriptors' in the syllabus. A 'How far?' question is based around one of those descriptors and is set to find out how much you know about the subject.

You can get up to 4 marks for identifying relevant points in the source and explaining them.

You can get up to 7 marks for including accurate and relevant information from your own knowledge.

The secret of success is to write a **balanced** answer.

First of all you must spot relevant information in the source, quote from it briefly to help answer the question and explain how your selection of words from the source helps to answer the question. Try to explain what the point of view of the author of the source is.

Secondly, throughout your answer, you must use your own knowledge. The source will never tell the full story so you are expected to use recall to develop your answer further. In all evaluation questions you **must** use recalled information to add relevant points or explanations to support and explain your answer.

For examples of answers to 'How far?' questions see pages 60, 62, 66, 88, 92 and 96.

TOP EXAM TIP

Both the 'How far?' and 'How fully?' questions are worth 10 marks so the answers should be roughly the same length, ideally about two sides of A4 paper.

How to answer the 'How fully?' question

There are four issues within each special study topic. A 'How fully?' question is based on one of the four issues. The rules about how to answer this type of question are the same as answering a 'How far?' question so look back at the information about answering 'How far?' questions. The only difference is in the topic of the question. The 'How far?' question will ask about **part** of an issue. The 'How fully?' question will ask about the whole issue.

For examples of answers to 'How fully?' questions see pages 59, 65, 69, 86, 90 and 94.

TOP EXAM TIP

In all the four question types it may help you to start by saying a source is **partly** useful or helpful in giving information. After all, a brief source extract can never give the whole story! By writing that sources agree partly, or a source explains something partly, or a source is partly useful, you open up the question.

- First of all you can select information from the source and develop that with your recall.

- Secondly, although the source will provide relevant information, it will not give all the information you need to lead towards a balanced conclusion. Your task is to include other information relevant to the answer from your own knowledge in order to provide a full answer.

- Finally, you can end with a short conclusion that provides a balanced answer to the question by reminding a marker that you have selected relevant points from the source that **partly** help to answer the question but that you have also included your own knowledge to provide a more balanced and thorough answer.

More information on the different types of question, with examples of answers, can be found in Leckie & Leckie's Higher History Grade Booster, *also written by John A. Kerr.*

The practice papers

Paper 1

Each year the three essay questions on each topic in Paper 1 will be based on three issues taken from the syllabus. The three issues selected will change each year.

In this book the questions in Examination Paper A, Paper 1 are based on issues 1, 3 and 5.

The questions in Examination Paper B, Paper 1 are based on issues 2, 4 and 6.

In the final section of the book you will find marking advice. This includes advice on Structure, and on Knowledge and Analysis points that would be appropriate to include in the answers to the questions.

Read this!

The marking advice does not provide all the relevant information and analysis points that could be included but it does provide a wide selection of information that you **could** use. The important point here is that you **do not have to use all** the information in the marking advice. A perfectly good answer could be written by using a selection of the material included in each section of marking advice.

The marking advice for Paper 1 provides for each question:

- the essay title;
- a clear statement of what the topic and task are;
- direct advice about a suitable context for the essay;
- a list of main points that signpost the main points that you could develop and what your main arguments will be;
- a list of relevant factual information that would gain K marks;
- a suggestion of points that could help gain A marks;
- top exam tips to help construct effective answers to the different types of question.

Paper 2
Each year, Paper 2 will contain sets of four questions assessing the four different issues in each of the five Scottish history topics. Remember, you only have to answer one set of four questions about **one** Scottish history topic. All issues will be assessed every year. The type of question used to assess each issue will vary year on year. For example, a 'How useful?' question may be used to assess issue 1 one year but the following year the same type of question might be used to assess issue 4. The topics asked about will reflect their order of appearance in the exam paper so the first question will be linked to issue 1, the second linked to issue 2 and so on.

The marking schemes for Paper 2 provide:

- four questions that are identical in style to those in the SQA exam;
- a step-by-step explanation of what to write in each section of each answer;
- suggestions for possible information that could be used to develop the answer;
- top exam tips to help construct effective answers to the different types of questions.

Examination A

History   Higher

Practice Papers   Time: 1 hour 20 minutes   **Examination A**
For SQA Exams   **Paper 1**

Answer **two** questions, **one** from Historical Study: British History and **one** from
Historical Study: European and World History.

Each question is worth **20 marks**.

Leckie ✕ Leckie
Scotland's leading educational publishers

HISTORICAL STUDY: BRITISH HISTORY

Answer ONE question. Each question is worth 20 marks.

Britain 1851–1951

1. To what extent were economic and social changes the reasons for Britain becoming more democratic between the 1850s and 1918?

2. How important was the Great War in winning votes for women?

3. How successfully did the Liberal reforms 1906–1914 deal with the problem of poverty?

HISTORICAL STUDY: EUROPEAN AND WORLD HISTORY

Answer ONE question. Each question is worth 20 marks.

Germany 1815–1939

4. To what extent were economic factors the main reason for the growth of national feeling in Germany between 1815 and 1850?

5. To what extent was lack of popular support the main obstacle to German unification before 1850?

6. 'Without Adolf Hitler the Nazis would never have achieved power in Germany.' How valid is that opinion about the importance of Hitler's leadership to the rise of the Nazis by 1933?

USA 1918–1968

7. To what extent was fear of crime the main reason why attitudes towards immigrants changed in the early 1920s?

8. To what extent was the overproduction of goods by American manufacturers the main reason for the depression of the 1930s?

9. 'The Double V Campaign and the experience of World War Two marked the beginning of serious demands for civil rights in America.' How accurate is that statement about the growth of the civil rights campaigns after 1945?

Appeasement and the Road to War, to 1939

10. To what extent were aggressive fascist foreign policies caused by economic difficulties in the 1930s?

11. To what extent was Britain's adoption of a policy of appeasement between 1936 and 1938 due to pressure from public opinion?

12. 'Munich was a triumph for British policy, not a failure.' How far can that view be supported?

History

Higher

Practice Papers
For SQA Exams

Time: 1 hour 25 minutes

Examination A
Paper 2

Answer **all** the questions on **one** special topic.

You can get up to **30 marks** for this paper.

THE WARS OF INDEPENDENCE, 1286–1328

Source A is adapted from *The Scottish Wars of Independence 1286–1328* by Andy MacPhee (2010).

King Edward of England was the young Margaret's great grand uncle. Naturally he was interested in her wellbeing, but he also saw a way of expanding his influence over Scotland. The issue of overlordship had long hung over relations between England and Scotland but had lain quiet during the reign of Alexander III. Now, with Alexander's death, Edward suggested a marriage between the young Margaret and his own son, who was then only ten years old. Both sides seemed happy and the Treaty of Birgham, signed in 1290, agreed that a marriage would take place between Margaret and young Prince Edward. The positive results of a marriage were that the threat of civil war in Scotland vanished and the simmering issue of overlordship and boundary disputes would be solved.

However, the Guardians were well aware that they might be giving away Scotland's freedom by agreeing to the marriage so they included several important sections designed to protect Scotland's freedoms. The Guardians intended the Treaty of Birgham to keep Scotland separate and free from control by England.

Source B was written by John Balliol from Kincardine in 1296.

John, by the grace of God king of Scotland, greets all who shall see or hear this letter. In view of the fact that through bad and wrong advice and our own foolishness we have in many ways gravely displeased and angered our lord Edward by the grace of God king of England, in that while we still owed him fealty and homage we made an alliance with the king of France against him … we have defied our lord the king of England and have withdrawn ourselves from his homage and fealty by renouncing our homage … we have sent our men into his land of England to burn, loot, murder and commit other wrongs and have fortified the land of Scotland against him … for all these reasons the king of England entered the realm of Scotland and conquered it by force despite the army we sent against him, something he had a right to do as lord of his fee.

Therefore acting of our own free will we have surrendered the land of Scotland and all its people with the homage of them all to him.

Source C is from a letter sent by Andrew Moray and William Wallace to the merchants of Lübeck, written in October 1297.

Andrew of Moray and William Wallace, leaders of the army of the kingdom of Scotland, and of the community of the realm, to their wise and discreet beloved friends the mayors and common people of Lübeck and of Hamburg, greeting and increasing sincere affection. We have been told by trustworthy merchants of the kingdom of Scotland that you are considerate, helpful and well disposed in all cases and matters affecting us and our merchants and we are therefore more obliged to give you our thanks and a worthy repayment: to this end we willingly enter into an undertaking with you, asking you to have it announced to your merchants that they can have safe access to all ports of the Scottish Kingdom with their merchandise, because the Kingdom of Scotland, thanks be to God, has been recovered by war from the power of the English.

Fare well. Given at Haddington in Scotland, 11 October 1297

Source D is adapted from a recent textbook about the Battle of Bannockburn.

The Scots won at Bannockburn because of careful planning. Bruce was unsure if a battle was really necessary and made his plans so that the Scots could vanish into the forests if necessary rather than face a large, confident and strong English army.

Scottish control over the high road to Stirling was vital for victory and before the battle the Scots dug potts in and around the road to force the English to look for other ways to reach the castle. It soon became obvious that the only alternative route was across boggy ground unsuited to the English cavalry.

On the other hand the Scots were well trained. The Scottish schiltrons were mobile and were used to attack as well as defence. By keeping the schiltrons pushing forward the Scots gave the English no room to move or to regroup. Bruce also knew how to use his cavalry as a force ready to react to any threat from English archers. Finally, Bruce's leadership was vital. He is credited with using the 'small folk' to charge at a crucial moment of the battle, thereby demoralising the English.

Source E is from *A History of Military Defeats* by Alexander Foggo.

King Edward II lacked his father's skill and military 'awareness'. As battle with the Scots approached, the English chain of command was still unclear. The reasons for such foolhardy directions are still not certain.

The English army was well equipped with scouts who knew the terrain well, so why then did Edward's forces march onto boggy land on which their room for manoeuvre was severely restricted by the Bannock Burn and the Firth of Forth?

When the second day of the battle began, the English cavalry advanced on the Scots expecting an easy victory. Why had they learned nothing from the errors of the first day of the battle or from their earlier victory at Falkirk? They knew that the way to deal with schiltrons was to use archers, defended by cavalry, and send wave after wave of arrows into the packed masses of Scots.

The English army was huge compared to the Scots, as was the experience and ability of the English forces. We are left with the conclusion that the Battle of Bannockburn was not so much won by the Scots as lost by the English.

THE WARS OF INDEPENDENCE, 1286–1328

Answer all the following questions *Marks*

1. How fully does Source A illustrate the issues that arose as a result of the succession problem in Scotland 1286–1292?
   Use the source and recalled knowledge. **10**

2. How far does Source B explain the reasons for Edward's subjugation of the Scots in 1296?
   Use the source and recalled knowledge. **10**

3. How useful is Source C in showing the importance of William Wallace to Scottish resistance against the English?
   In reaching a conclusion you should refer to:
   • *the origin and possible purpose of the source;*
   • *the content of the source;*
   • *recalled knowledge.* **5**

4. To what extent do Sources D and E agree in their opinions about why the Scots won the Battle of Bannockburn?
   Compare the sources overall and in detail. **5**
   (30)

THE TREATY OF UNION, 1689–1740

Source A is from *The Union of Scotland and England* by P. H. Scott (1979).

The Scottish Parliament turned to measures designed to restore Scottish trade from the effects of a century of neglect and discrimination. In 1695, it passed an Act for a company trading to Africa and the Indies. This was the Company of Scotland which, as the first of its ventures, decided to settle a colony at Darien. William, as King of Scotland, agreed to the Act but as King of England, he was obliged to do all he could to sabotage and oppose the efforts of the Company. When the Darien scheme failed many asked how a country could succeed when its own Head of State actively opposed its interests. This criticism came hard on the heels of the concern over William's possible involvement in the Glencoe massacre. At this critical moment, when relations between the two countries were as bad as they had ever been, a dynastic accident offered a solution. The last child of the future Queen Anne died in 1700. In 1701, the English Parliament, without consultation with Scotland, passed the Act of Settlement, passing the succession after Anne to the Electress Sophia of Hanover.

Source B is from the Earl of Seafield's letters.

My reasons for joining with England on good terms were these: that the kingdom of England is a Protestant kingdom and that, therefore, the joining with them was a security for our religion. Secondly, England has trade and other advantages to give us, which no other kingdom could offer. Thirdly, England has freedom and liberty, and joining with them was the best way to secure that to us; and fourthly, I saw no other method for securing peace, the two kingdoms being in the same island, and foreign assistance was both dangerous to ourselves and England. Therefore, I was for the treaty.

Source C is from a petition against the proposed union sent from Stirling Town Council in November 1707.

We desire that true peace and friendship be always cultivated with our neighbour England, upon just and honourable terms ... Yet we judge that going into this Treaty will bring a burden of taxation upon this land, which freedom of trade will never repay ... Scotland would still be under the regulations of the English in the Parliament of Britain, who may if they please discourage the most valuable branches of our trade, if we in any way are seen to interfere with their own. It will ruin our manufactories, our religion, laws and liberties. As a result, one of the most ancient nations so long and so gloriously defended will be suppressed. Our parliament and all that is dear to us will be extinguished.

Source D is from the Memoirs of Lockhart of Carnwath, written in 1714.

The ministers were concerned about the government of the Kirk, and roared against the wicked union from their pulpits, and sent addresses against it from several presbyteries and the Assembly. But no sooner did Parliament pass an act for the security of the Kirk than most of their zeal was cooled, and many of them changed their tune and preached in favour of it. But the truth of the matter lies here: a sum of money was necessary to be distributed amongst the Scots. And this distribution of it amongst the proprietors of the Company of Scotland was the best way of bribing a nation ... alas it had the desired effect.

Source E is adapted from *Scotland's Relations with England* by William Ferguson (1977).

As it was, once the contents of the treaty had been leaked, nearly every sector of the Scottish nation found something objectionable in the proposed union. The Jacobites, rightly enough from their standpoint, saw it as a deadly blow to the hopes of the exiled Stuarts. The Episcopalians, most of whom favoured the Stuarts, were afraid that the union would secure Presbyterianism. The Presbyterians welcomed the Protestant succession, but feared that, under the union, bishops would again be thrust upon the Church of Scotland. Strangely, the offer of free trade gained little enthusiasm in many of the royal burghs, including Glasgow. The merchants of Scotland feared they would be swamped by English trade and new restrictive laws passed by the new British parliament that was in reality the English parliament. They did not believe the union offered entry to the shelter of an empire the expansion and defence of which the Scots themselves were to contribute to with their labour and lives.

THE TREATY OF UNION, 1689–1740

Answer all of the following questions

Marks

1. How far does Source A explain incidents leading to worsening relations with England?
   Use the source and recalled knowledge.

   10

2. To what extent do Sources B and C agree in their attitudes towards union?
   Compare the sources overall and in detail.

   5

3. How useful is Source D as evidence of the methods used to pass the Treaty of Union?
   In reaching a conclusion you should refer to:
   - *the origin and possible purpose of the source;*
   - *the content of the source;*
   - *recalled knowledge.*

   5

4. How fully does Source E summarise feelings in Scotland about the effects of the union up to 1740?
   Use the source and recalled knowledge.

   10

   (30)

SCOTLAND AND THE IMPACT OF THE GREAT WAR, 1914–1928

Source A is from *Everyman at War* (1930).

For a whole week before the Battle of Loos, our artillery were bombarding the German trenches night and day, smashing up the barbed wire. On September 24th, 1915, my battalion marched up the communication trenches under a heavy shell-fire from the enemy guns.

Early in the morning the snipers were at their posts, ready to put a bullet into any German that happened to look over the top.

Then it was over the top and the best of luck. Men were lying about in hundreds, some blown to pieces lying mangled in shell holes.

Making our way through gaps in the German barbed wire, we were held up by machine gun fire and had to try and dig ourselves in with our entrenching tools. Suddenly we got the order to retire and then saw the Germans sending forward strong reinforcements, and it is a wonder that any of us had the luck to get back.

Only about 50 returned out of the 500 that advanced too far over the hill. After midnight, our battalion was taken to a little village not far behind the line. There we had breakfast and a wash-up.

Source B is from the socialist newspaper *Forward* for 20 November 1915.

Defence of the Realm Act
John Maclean fined £5

Full report of trial.

Last Wednesday John Maclean of the British Socialist Party was charged at Glasgow under the Defence of the Realm Act with having, in the course of addressing a crowd of people in Bath Street, Glasgow, made a statement likely to prejudice recruitment for His Majesty's forces. He said, 'I have been a socialist for fifteen years! God damn the army and all other armies!' He also spoke in Pollockshaws Road saying, 'any soldier who shot another soldier in this war is a murderer'.

A witness was asked if he thought that Maclean was telling people they should not join the army because they would become murderers. The witness replied, 'I do sir.'

The court was told that the crowd became menacing towards Maclean but a steward said, 'To hell with them John, just go on.' At this point the police came forward and arrested Maclean.

Sheriff Lee said that he was dealing with an exceptional law passed not to secure loyalty of the citizens but security for the kingdom.

Source C is from the *Glasgow Herald* for 14 April 1923.

This weekend is witnessing emigration from the Hebrides on a scale comparable only to that experienced in the early 1880s.

Thirty families, numbering some 400 souls, are leaving Benbecula, South Uist and Barra to seek a future for themselves and their children on the land of Alberta, Canada. This scheme was initiated by the Rev. Father McDonnell. Another priest visited Canada and reported on the prospects to the intending emigrants who, it is understood, will be accompanied to their new home by two priests. The emigration is being carried out by arrangement with the Canadian Pacific Railway Company. Their ship, the *Marloch*, will early this afternoon sail from Greenock with about 700 Scottish emigrants, many of them of the tradesman class, going out to seek employment in Canada or take up work on the land.

Next weekend a second party will sail from Stornoway with between 400 and 500 persons. They are going out with the encouragement of the government of Ontario, Canada.

Source D is from the Department of Agriculture and Fisheries, 1920–1930 (files AF 51/212, pp 20, 22, 23, 26).

There is a distinct change of feeling in the Western Islands regarding immigration in these post war years caused by encouraging reports being received from crofting families who have gone out from Barra and South Uist. The other reason for this change of attitude is the readiness on the part of some priests to consider emigration as a means of improving the condition of the people and escaping unemployment and destitution at home. It is most desirable that the Scottish Office should not overlook the idea of land settlement in the Dominions and in particular in Canada. The Canadian government is apparently willing to do its part. A deputation of two South Uist crofters and a priest from Barra left for the dominion of Canada at the expense of the Canadian government to select the most suitable localities for settling the folk from the Hebrides.

Source E is from *Scotland and the Impact of the Great War* by John A. Kerr (2010).

In 1918 the Labour Party's election manifesto promised to fight for the complete restoration of the land of Scotland to the Scottish people but these proposals did not catch the public's imagination or support. In the 1920s all three major parties actively supported the Union, and Home Rule bills in parliament in 1924 and 1927 went nowhere.

Nevertheless there were some who continued to campaign actively for an independent Scotland and in the 1920s economic distress made more people listen to the arguments for independence.

Radical nationalists wanted to resist the erosion of Scottish culture and Scottish identity by the spread of Englishness in all aspects of life. Artists, writers and poets, such as Hugh MacDiarmid, styled themselves as a Scottish literary renaissance and took pride in their attacks on those who, in their view, had sold out to England.

In May 1928 the National Party of Scotland was founded but its leaders, Roland Muirhead and John McCormick, received only 3000 votes in the 1929 general election, less than 5% of the vote in each constituency.

SCOTLAND AND THE IMPACT OF THE GREAT WAR, 1914–1928

Answer all the following questions   *Marks*

1. How far does Source A show the experience of Scots on the Western Front?
    Use the source and recalled knowledge.   **10**

2. How useful is Source B as evidence of attitudes about recruitment and the
    Defence of the Realm Act?
    In reaching a conclusion you should refer to:
    *   *the origin and possible purpose of the source;*
    *   *the content of the source;*
    *   *recalled knowledge.*   **5**

3. To what extent do Sources C and D agree about post-war emigration from
    Scotland?
    Compare the sources overall and in detail.   **5**

4. How fully does Source E explain the impact of the war on political developments
    in Scotland?
    Use the source and recalled knowledge.   **10**
                                                                                (30)

Examination B

History   Higher

Practice Papers   Time: 1 hour 20 minutes   **Examination B**
For SQA Exams   **Paper 1**

Answer **two** questions, **one** from Historical Study: British History and **one** from
Historical Study: European and World History.

Each question is worth **20 marks**.

Scotland's leading educational publishers

HISTORICAL STUDY: BRITISH HISTORY

Answer ONE question. Each question is worth 20 marks.

Britain 1851–1951

1. To what extent did Britain make progress towards democracy between the 1850s and 1918?

2. How far was concern over poverty the main reason for the Liberal government's decision to introduce social reforms between 1906 and 1914?

3. To what extent did the Labour government of 1945–1951 deal successfully with the social problems facing Britain after World War Two?

HISTORICAL STUDY: EUROPEAN AND WORLD HISTORY

Answer ONE question. Each question is worth 20 marks.

Germany 1815–1939

4. How accurate is it to claim that between 1815 and 1850 there was a real growth in German nationalism?

5. 'Bismarck's leadership was vital to the creation of a united Germany by 1871.' How accurate is that opinion?

6. How far was the use of fear, force and threats responsible for the survival of the Nazi state between 1933 and 1939?

USA 1918–1968

7. How far was the Ku Klux Klan responsible for the lack of progress towards civil rights for black Americans in the years up to 1941?

8. How effectively did the New Deal achieve its aims?

9. How far had the aims of the civil rights movement resulted in improvements in the lives of black Americans by 1968?

Appeasement and the Road to War, to 1939

10. To what extent did fascist powers use tactics of threats and bullying to pursue their foreign policy aims in the years after 1933?

11. How far is it true to say that the policy of appeasement was a complete failure in containing the spread of fascist aggression up to March 1938?

12. 'The crisis over Poland triggered World War Two.' How valid is this view?

History

Higher

Practice Papers
For SQA Exams

Time: 1 hour 25 minutes

Examination B
Paper 2

Answer **all** the questions on **one** special topic.

You can get up to **30 marks** for this paper.

Leckie✕Leckie

Scotland's leading educational publishers

THE WARS OF INDEPENDENCE, 1286–1328

Source A is from a letter written by William Fraser, Bishop of St Andrews, to King Edward in 1290.

To Lord Edward, King of England from William, minister of the church of Saint Andrew in Scotland.

There is a sorrowful rumour that our Lady Margaret of Norway is dead, on which account the kingdom of Scotland is disturbed and the community distracted. On hearing the rumour, Sir Robert de Bruce came with a great army to Perth but what he intends to do we know not. But the Earls of Mar and Atholl are already collecting their army and there is fear of a general war and a great slaughter of men.

If it turns out that our Lady Margaret has departed this life, let your Excellency approach the border with an army to help save the shedding of blood and to set over Scotland a king who of right ought to have the succession, so long that he follows your advice. If Sir John Balliol comes to your presence we advise you to speak with him so that your honour and advantage be preserved.

Given at Leuchars, in the year of our Lord, 1290.

Source B is adapted from *The Scottish Wars of Independence 1286–1328* by Andy MacPhee (2010).

It was the prospect of a foreign war that caused rebellion in Scotland. In 1294 Edward was preparing to make war in France in order to pursue his ambitions there. As usual the English king summoned his feudal vassals and King John was ordered to appear to fight for Edward, in much the same way as the great earls of England were. The assumption that Scotland was to be treated the same as the great estates as England was bad enough, but the assumption that the Scots were to fight against France, Scotland's largest trading partner, was worse. Added to this were the demands for taxes from the Scottish nobility to fund and prepare for the war. It is no wonder that the Scottish nobles were willing to revolt against Edward.

In 1295 six new Guardians were appointed by the community of the realm to defy King Edward. They sent envoys to the King of France and at the beginning of 1296 a treaty against Edward was agreed.

Source C is from a lecture given by Janet Stenhouse.

King Edward I led his army north in 1298 and faced Wallace at Falkirk. Wallace should have avoided battle against the superior English forces but he had seriously misjudged them. Edward's 'secret weapon' was the Welsh archers whose arrows ripped apart the Scottish schiltrons.

Later historians said that Wallace had been deliberately abandoned by Scots noblemen including the Comyns who deserted the battlefield. However, in reality the Scottish nobility on horseback were simply outnumbered by the English cavalry.

Wallace's defeat at Falkirk ruined his image of invincibility. Wallace was forced to resign his title as Guardian of Scotland and the Scottish nobility resumed their old role as Guardians of the kingdom. In the years that followed Wallace's defeat it seemed as if Scottish resistance had crumbled. The French ended their alliance with Scotland and in 1304 the Scots leaders – all apart from Wallace – surrendered and recognised Edward as their overlord. Wallace was now alone and refused to compromise. The English king was prepared to bargain with the Scottish leaders but he wanted Wallace dead. Wallace was now an embarrassment for the Scottish leadership. The Scots were prepared to do a deal with Edward and Wallace was like a guilty conscience. For both sides, it would be better if Wallace no longer existed!

Source D was written in the *Lanercost Chronicle* soon after the Battle of Falkirk.

The victory of Falkirk was granted to the enemy through the treachery of the Scots nobles. William Wallace saw by this and other strong evidence the obvious wickedness of the Comyns and those who were in league with them. He therefore chose to serve with the common people than be set over the Scots' nobles as a leader. So not long after the battle of Falkirk, at the water of Forth, he, of his own accord, resigned his office and charge that he held of Guardian. Wallace kept alive the hopes of his countrymen and bravely resisted the English when other cowards in Scotland knelt in surrender to the English invaders.

Source E is from John of Fordun, *Chronicle of the Scottish Nation* (1350).

In the year 1311, King Robert having put all his enemies to flight at every place he came to and having taken their fortresses and levelled them to the ground twice entered England and wasted it, carrying off untold booty and making huge havoc with fire and sword. Thus the English nation, which had unrighteously wracked many a man, was now by God's righteous judgement made to undergo awful scourgings and whereas it was once victorious, now it sank vanquished and groaning.

On January 8, the town of Perth was taken with the strong hand by King Robert and the disloyal people both English and Scots were taken, dragged and slain with the sword. The king in his clemency spared the rabble and granted forgiveness to those that asked it but he destroyed the walls and ditches and consumed everything else with fire.

THE WARS OF INDEPENDENCE, 1286–1328

Answer all of the following questions

Marks

1. How useful is Source A as evidence of the problems caused by the death of the Maid of Norway?
   In reaching a conclusion you should refer to:
   • *the origin and possible purpose of the source;*
   • *the content of the source;*
   • *recalled knowledge.*   5

2. How fully does Source B show the changing relationship between John Balliol and Edward I?
   Use the source and recalled knowledge.   10

3. To what extent do Sources C and D agree about the reasons for defeat at Falkirk and continuing Scottish resistance?
   Compare the sources overall and in detail.   5

4. How far does Source E illustrate the reasons for Bruce's victory over his Scottish opponents?
   Use the source and recalled knowledge.   10

(30)

MIGRATION AND EMPIRE, 1830–1939

Source A is a Canadian Emigration Office poster from the 1920s.

Source B is from 'Here are the Lithuanians', a recent article by Myra Strachan.

After they arrived in Scotland, mostly at the port of Leith, the Lithuanians split into two groups, the Jewish immigrants settling in the Gorbals and the Catholic Lithuanians heading for the smelting works of North Ayrshire, the mines of West Lothian and, mainly, for the iron works and mines of Lanarkshire.

The Lithuanians were not made welcome in Scotland. They were seen as competition in the market for jobs, and employers were often accused of using them as strike-breakers. Not only were the newcomers obviously foreign, with little or no grasp of the English language, but many were also devoutly Catholic in a fiercely Presbyterian land.

Trade Unions were openly hostile, claiming that the newcomers' lack of English made them a danger at work. The Glasgow Trades Council declared the Lithuanians in Glengarnock as 'an evil' and wrote to the TUC demanding immigration controls to keep them out.

Source C is from a description of Scots immigrants to Ontario, Canada, written by a Church of England minister in the early nineteenth century.

I do not consider that the inhabitants of the islands of Scotland are well suited to the wants and needs of this colony. Their total ignorance of the English language makes it difficult to get employment for them, while their laziness and extremely filthy habits have not made a good impression on the British people already here. It would be better if such immigration was restricted at least since these wretches have little to offer this society. Indeed, it cannot be argued other than their arrival is having a most unwelcome and detrimental effect on the inhabitants of this colony.

Source D is from *The Emigrant Scot* by Jacqueline Tee.

Far from being 'lazy' and ignorant because they could not speak English, most Scots made a vital contribution to the development of the Empire. Scots had a reputation as good workers and most Scots could read and write, and spoke English.

Across the globe Scottish soldiers and explorers opened up the new colonies, defended colonists and in numerous conflicts extended the boundaries of the Empire from India to Canada and on to New Zealand.

Many immigrant Scots were determined to succeed and they adapted well to the harsh climates and difficult lands which they had experienced at home.

Scottish farming expertise was vital to the development of the Australian and New Zealand sheep-farming economy.

Other Scots were skilled tradesmen who were needed in America, Canada, Australia and New Zealand. Scots who were doctors, lawyers, engineers, accountants or architects were also in high demand. Finally, but not least, Scots missionaries brought to societies the word of God to 'dark continents' around the world.

Source E is from *The Scottish Nation* by Tom Devine (2000).

Italian 'colonies' grew up in the Gorbals in Glasgow, in Edinburgh's Grassmarket and Aberdeen's Castlegate.

The Italians in Scotland quickly became committed to the catering trade, with families owning and running ice cream parlours and fish and chip shops.

The Italians brought new consumer delights to the working-class areas of Scotland. 'Pokey hats' (ice cream cones) were always popular and fish suppers became the original fast food of the common man.

Those chip shops and ice cream cafés also stayed open late into the evening, long after their Scottish competitors had closed for the night. They were a huge attraction for young people who wanted somewhere to meet away from the family home.

These cafés attracted support from temperance groups who saw the ice cream parlours as a real and attractive alternative to the alcoholic temptations of the public house.

The Italian community attracted much less hostility from native Scots than the Catholic Irish or Lithuanians. The Italians offered a popular service. They were few in number and almost all worked in family-run businesses. They therefore posed little threat to native workers or wages.

It was an introspective community that had few social contacts with the rest of Scottish society. For many, the hope was eventually to return to Italy so any attempt at assimilation seemed pointless.

MIGRATION AND EMPIRE, 1830–1939

Marks

Answer all of the following questions

1. How useful is Source A as evidence of the push and pull factors influencing emigration from Scotland?
   In reaching a conclusion you should refer to:
   • *the origin and possible purpose of the source;*
   • *the content of the source;*
   • *recalled knowledge.*   **5**

2. How fully does Source B illustrate the experience of immigrants in Scotland?
   Use the source and recalled knowledge.   **10**

3. To what extent do Sources C and D disagree about the impact of Scots emigrants on the growth and development of the Empire?
   Compare the sources overall and in detail.   **5**

4. How far does Source E illustrate the contribution of immigrants to Scottish society and culture?
   Use the source and recalled knowledge.   **10**

   (30)

SCOTLAND AND THE IMPACT OF THE GREAT WAR, 1914–1928

Source A is a recruitment poster used in Scotland in the autumn of 1914.

Source B was spoken by Grace Kennedy, from Glasgow, quoted in Ian MacDougall, *Voices from War* (1995).

I married during the war, in 1917. I married a man who was gassed and came back from the war. I went into a single room apartment in Govan and then got a job at an engineering works.

During the war years there were people getting put out of their homes because they couldn't pay the rent. The landlords decided to put the rent up by about 50%. It was supposed to be for repairs. Then we had nine months of a Rent Strike. Well, quite a lot got into difficulties at this time, money difficulties I mean. A lot of folk who stopped paying rent didnae save the rent money for when they would have to pay. Some of us saved our rent and had then to pay a certain amount in arrears. But then the Rent Restriction Act was brought in and made it easier. I think it was due to the work of Baillie Mary Barbour particularly and the women that the Rent Restriction Act was brought into being.

Source C is from an interview with Charlie Young, a Scot who lived in London during World War One.

When I came back after the war my family told me how bad it had been. You see, us being an island hardly any food could get through, because German U-boats were sinking our food convoys. My family lived on bones from the butcher made into soups. And stale bread. When some food did get delivered to the shops everyone for miles around crowded round the place. The queues stretched for miles, and if you were old or unsteady on your feet you stood no chance. Many, especially children, died of starvation. Food riots were very common.

Source D is from the *War Memoirs* of David Lloyd George.

So far as the vast bulk of the population was concerned, this rationing system ensured a regular and sufficient food supply; and it made it possible for those in charge to calculate with some precision how best they could make the stocks of available food-stuffs go round fairly. Although there was a degree of scarcity, we were never faced with famine or actual privation. The steady improvement in our national health figures during and after the war shows that compulsory temperance in eating was in general more beneficial than harmful in its effects. Credit is due to our people for the loyal manner in which they submitted themselves to these strange and unwelcome restrictions. Without general goodwill it would have been impossible to make the regulations effective.

Source E is from *Red Clydeside* by Iain Maclean.

In the eyes of many in Britain, Glasgow during the First World War gained the reputation of being a centre of socialist if not communist ideas, a hotbed of revolution. By 1922, or perhaps earlier, the city had acquired the nickname 'Red Clydeside'. The reality of Red Clydeside was smaller, and more mixed, than the myth. During the First World War the core of it was a skilled workers' protest against 'dilution', which meant bringing in unskilled men and women to do parts of skilled trade jobs. Some of the socialist leaders, including John Maclean, opposed the war; others, including David Kirkwood, did not.

In the 1922 General Election ten Labour MPs were elected for Glasgow constituencies. Before leaving together from St Enoch Station to take their seats at Westminster, they had a send-off where the audience sang 'The Red Flag'. Red Clydeside nurtured some people who later became prominent in the Labour Party or the Independent Labour Party (ILP).

SCOTLAND AND THE IMPACT OF THE GREAT WAR, 1914–1928

Answer all of the following questions

Marks

1. How useful is Source A as evidence of why so many young Scots joined the army in 1914?
   In reaching a conclusion you should refer to:
   • *the origin and possible purpose of the source;*
   • *the content of the source;*
   • *recalled knowledge.* **5**

2. How fully does Source B illustrate the impact of the war on Scottish society?
   Use the source and recalled knowledge. **10**

3. To what extent do Sources C and D agree about the effects of rationing on Scottish society during the war?
   Compare the sources overall and in detail. **5**

4. How far does Source E show the impact of the war on the growth of radicalism, the ILP and Red Clydeside?
   Use the source and recalled knowledge. **10**

   (30)

Answers

Britain 1851–1951

> **1.** To what extent were economic and social changes the reasons for Britain becoming more democratic between the 1850s and 1918?

TOPIC AND TASK

The topic of this question is the growth of democracy in Britain between the 1850s and 1918.

The task of this question is to:

1. Explain why social and economic changes led to political changes in Britain.
2. Explain other reasons why Britain became more democratic.
3. Reach a balanced conclusion that directly answers the question.

> **TOP EXAM TIP**
>
> This is one of two very different questions about democracy. To answer this question you must be able to explain **why** Britain became more democratic. It is **not** enough to describe what happened and what laws were passed to make Britain a democracy. That is a different type of question.

STRUCTURE

Context example

In 1850 only one in six adult males could vote yet by 1918 the vote had been extended to all males aged 21 or over and some women aged 30 or over. In that time Britain had undergone many economic and social changes, all of which had in some way created pressure for political changes.

Introduction points to signpost:

- The effects of social and economic changes in Britain, such as industrialisation, urbanisation, spread of easy transport, growth of middle- and working-class identity.
- Changing political ideology in the nineteenth century.
- Winning political advantage as a reason for reform.
- The influence of pressure groups.
- The effect of the Great War.

THE DEVELOPMENT SECTION

To gain K marks you must include accurate and relevant factual detail, such as:

Social and economic change

- The voting reforms of 1867, 1884, 1918.
- The growth of cities (urbanisation) and the changing distribution of population.
- Increasing wealth and importance of middle-class businessmen.
- Growing influence of working-class organisations.
- The growth and spread of railways.
- The growth of mass education and greater literacy.
- Increasing popularity of cheap newspapers and spread of public libraries.

To gain A marks you must **use** your information to link directly to the question. In this case that means you must be able to explain the link between your factual knowledge and the reasons why Britain became more democratic by 1918. Analysis/argument points about social and economic change could include:

- Changes in population distribution were important because these changes led to demands for fairer representation in parliament and the redistribution of parliamentary seats – redistribution of seats in 1867, 1885, 1918.
- Middle-class businessmen became important wealth creators and demanded better representation in parliament.
- The growth of cities (urbanisation) led to growth of class identity and demands for fairer representation in parliament.
- The working classes became more politically aware thanks to education for all and cheap, popular newspapers. At the same time there was a realisation by those in power that preventing any change at all would simply increase pressure for even greater change. It therefore became necessary to consider giving the working classes the vote.
- The organisation of working classes into trades unions, combined with the ideology of socialism, created more pressure for change.
- As the working classes became more skilled and more 'respectable' they were no longer seen as a potentially violent mob. Reform was no longer seen as a threat.
- On the other hand, as pressure groups became larger and better organised, parliament saw some political change as a way of preventing demands for more extreme change.
- The spread of literacy, access to information and railways helped people become more aware of political issues.

To balance your answer you must also include other K mark reasons for change and these could include:
- Changing political ideas and attitudes.
- The death of former PM Palmerston.
- Hopes for political advantage.
- The impact of demonstrations by the Reform League and Reform Union.
- Details of the Reform Acts of 1867, 1884, 1918.
- The campaigns of the Suffragists and Suffragettes.
- The growth of socialism and creation of the Labour Party.
- The impact of the Great War.

Analysis/argument points for those other reasons could include:
- New political ideas and changing attitudes during the nineteenth century increased support and acceptance of democracy. This was encouraged by struggles for liberalism and nationalism spreading across Europe.
- The death of former PM Palmerston represented the changing tone of politics. Palmerston represented the older class of politicians who opposed all change. His death removed that automatic resistance to reform.
- Hopes for political advantage – the 1867 Reform Act was passed by the Conservatives who hoped to gain support from the new voters.
- The impact of demonstrations by the Reform League and Reform Union, such as 'intimidation Monday', might be over-exaggerated, but they did gain attention for reform ideas.
- The campaigns of the Suffragettes and Suffragists had varied success in gaining support for the cause of votes for women but the issue was kept firmly in the headlines.
- The growth of socialist groups led eventually to the creation of the Labour Party. That gave the working classes an important political voice for change.
- The impact of the Great War created a readiness to accept political reform. Partly as a result of women's war work, the political consequences of conscription and changing attitudes of politicians, parliament was ready to accept further parliamentary reform by 1918.

OVERALL

Overall, economic and social changes had a big effect both on demands for reform and also on the willingness of political parties to carry out that reform. However, other factors, such as political parties trying to win advantages for themselves and the effects of the Great War, also led to significant changes that made Britain more democratic between the 1850s and 1918.

> 2. How important was the Great War in winning votes for women?

TOPIC AND TASK

The topic of this question is the campaign for votes for women.

The task of this question is to:
1. Explain why the Great War had an effect on the campaign for votes for women.
2. Consider the importance of other reasons why women were given the vote in 1918.
3. Reach a balanced conclusion that directly answers the question.

STRUCTURE

Context example

By 1900 the role and status of women in society were changing, but women still had no national political voice. The NUWSS had campaigned peacefully since the 1880s but not much had changed. In 1903 the Women's Social and Political Union was created to push for more rapid change.

Introduction points to signpost:
- Changing role of women by 1914.
- Differing campaigns of the WSPU and NUWSS.
- Effects of Great War: changing role of women during the war.
- Effects of Great War: differing reasons for the 1918 Representation of the People Act.

THE DEVELOPMENT SECTION

To gain K marks you must include accurate and relevant factual detail, such as:

The effects of the Great War
- Women's war work – for example over 700 000 women employed in munitions.
- Women worked in many other areas of the war effort.
- Main women's organisations suspended their campaigns on the outbreak of war.
- WSPU actively urged men to join the armed forces and encouraged women to demand 'the right to serve'.
- NUWSS continued to use war work, e.g. sponsored ambulances, to demonstrate women's responsibility and importance to the war effort.
- War led to introduction of conscription, which led to the view that all men who had served in the armed forces should get the vote.

- Politicians were anxious to enfranchise more men who had fought in the war but had lost their residency qualification – easy to 'add on' women in legislation which was happening anyway.

Other factors
- Social change – in pre-war years women were increasingly active in public affairs – further change was inevitable.
- Role of the NUWSS – persuasive campaign of meetings, pamphlets, petitions.
- NUWSS had 53 000 members in 1914.
- Role of WSPU – publicity for campaign but much of the publicity was negative.
- Representation of the People Act 1918 – votes for some women aged 30 or over.

Analysis/argument points could include:

The effects of the Great War
- Women clearly gained respect during the war and that counterbalanced the negative publicity caused by the earlier Suffragette campaign.
- Women's war efforts were important in changing the opinion of political opponents such as PM Asquith.
- Public support gained by women 'doing their bit' during war.
- The traditional view is that women were given the vote as a reward for efforts during the war – a 'thank you'. However, in 1918, the vote was given to women aged 30 and over. The munition workers were largely young, single women below 30 – they did not get the vote. Therefore the role of women's war work in causing change is a debatable point. The war provided the opportunity for government to change its position without losing face.
- Reform of the franchise in 1918 to extend the vote to more men and some women would not have happened without war.
- The reform of 1918 was regarded as a victory for the suffrage movements but women were still not the political equals of men.

Other factors
- Social change – in pre-war years women were increasingly active in public affairs making further change inevitable. Historian Martin Pugh argues that women's active participation in local councils, boards of guardians and other organisations made it increasingly difficult to justify their exclusion from national elections.
- Many MPs accepted the principle of women's suffrage.
- The WSPU lost support because of the tactics and methods they adopted. However, the government was fearful of the Suffragette campaign restarting after the war. The reform of 1918 removed that possibility.
- Without the Suffragette campaign, the Liberal government might not have discussed the issue at all. The WSPU brought the issue of votes for women to crisis point and could not be ignored.
- The government was afraid that the suffragette campaign would revive if no reform was granted. In the post-war atmosphere of protest and revolution (abroad Russia and Germany, at home Red Clydeside) the government did not want more trouble.

OVERALL
War can be regarded as a catalyst that sped up progress towards votes for women but the move towards granting women the vote had started before the war.

---

3. How successfully did the Liberal reforms 1906–1914 deal with the problem of poverty?

TOPIC AND TASK
The topic of this question is the Liberal reforms of 1906–1914.

The task of this question is to:
1. Show that you know what the Liberal reforms were.
2. Use the detail of the reforms to decide whether or not they really did help to ease the problem of poverty.
3. Reach a balanced conclusion that directly answers the question.

STRUCTURE
Context example
By 1900 pressure on governments to do something about the problem of poverty was increasing. When the Liberals came to power in 1906 they began to introduce a series of social reforms aimed at helping the 'deserving poor'.

TOP EXAM TIP

This essay is **not** about why the reforms happened, so your context just sets the scene and lasts about two sentences. Do **not** get side-tracked into writing about the reasons for the reforms.

Introduction points to signpost:
- Reforms to help the young – Children's Charter.
- Reforms to help the old – pensions.

- Reforms to help the sick – National Insurance part 1.
- Reforms to help the unemployed – National Insurance part 2.

THE DEVELOPMENT SECTION

To gain K marks you must include accurate and relevant factual detail, such as:

Reforms to help the young
- Children's Charter – borstals, restrictions on buying tobacco and alcohol.
- School meals – permissive law allowed local authorities to feed poor children to assist education.
- Medical inspection 1907, treatment by 1912.

Reforms to help the old
- Old Age Pensions Act 1908.
- Pensions for over-70s if certain conditions met.

Reforms to help the sick
- National Insurance Act 1911 part 1.
- Benefits paid to workers who contributed to schemes.
- Part 1 – 'ninepence for fourpence'.
- Contributory scheme with individual paying 4 pence, the employer paying 3 pence and the government paying 2 pence per week.

Reforms to help the unemployed
- National Insurance Act 1911 part 2.
- Benefits paid to workers who contributed to schemes.
- Benefit covered seven types of employment.

Analysis/argument points could include:

Young
- Children's Charter really doing nothing new: just organising laws that already existed to protect children but not to ease their poverty.
- School meals – many local authorities did not provide service and school holidays returned children to hunger.
- Medical inspection 1907, at first nothing done to treat illness.

Old
- Pensions for over 70s but many poor seldom lived that long.
- Helped almost 1 million by 1914 but pension not for all.
- There were strict rules about who did and did not qualify for a pension.
- The amount paid still below Rowntree's poverty line.

Sickness
- Benefits limited and contributions reduced weekly wage of the poor.
- Only insured worker got medical help, not family.

Unemployed
- Insurance only covered some jobs and benefits only paid for limited time.

OVERALL

Churchill argued that reforms were only meant to help people to help themselves. He used the analogy of a drowning man who would be thrown a lifebelt and be expected to swim ashore rather than be given such help that the swimmer did not have to make any effort of his own.

Germany 1815–1939

> **4.** To what extent were economic factors the main reason for the growth of national feeling in Germany between 1815 and 1850?

TOPIC AND TASK

The topic of this question is **why** national feeling grew in Germany between 1815 and 1850.

The task of this question is to:

1. Explain how economic factors helped to increase national feeling in Germany during this time.
2. Explain the other reasons why national feeling grew.
3. Reach a balanced conclusion that directly answers the question.

TOP EXAM TIP

There are several questions on German unification that focus on the years 1815–1850. One of the questions is about the reasons for the growth of nationalism in Germany, another is about how much support for unification there really was in Germany before 1850. Finally, a third question is about the obstacles that existed on the path towards unification. Be very careful to gear your answer towards the precise question asked.

STRUCTURE

Context example

In 1800 there were around 400 separate states in what we now call Germany. When Napoleon invaded he reduced the number of states but he had no intention of uniting Germany. By 1815 Napoleon had been defeated and the former rulers of the German states returned to power with the intention of protecting the separate independence of the German states – with Austria's help.

Introduction points to signpost:

- Economic nationalism – the development in Prussia and its influence on national awareness.
- Political nationalism – growing support for nationalism and liberalism.
- Cultural nationalism – the increasing popularity of German cultural influences and awareness of German identity.

THE DEVELOPMENT SECTION

To gain K marks you must include accurate and relevant factual detail, such as:

Economic factors

- Prussia's gain of mineral-rich land in the Rhineland in 1815.
- The focus of growth and economic influence shifted to the North Sea trade area and the iron and coal resources of Prussia's new territory around the Rhineland.
- Growing demands for a more united trading area within Germany and the removal of obstacles to trade and economic growth.
- Austrian economic influence over Germany was becoming irrelevant.
- Prussia created customs union in 1818 that was to become the Zollverein. By 1836, 25 of the 39 German states had joined this economic free-trade area.
- Railway and road development spreading out from Prussia.

Political factors

- Ideas of the French Revolution appealed to the middle classes in the German states.
- German princes had stirred national feeling to help raise armies to drive out the French, aiding the sense of a common German identity with common goals.
- Creation of German Confederation raised some hopes.
- Austrian control of German Confederation – Metternich as focus of resentment.
- Resentment of Carlsbad Decrees.
- Wartburg festival protests.
- The Rhine Crisis of 1840. The growth of tensions and possibility of war with France.
- 1848 revolutions in Germany raised awareness even though they failed.

Cultural factors – 'Romanticism'

- Common language and culture shared by 25 million.
- Writers and thinkers (e.g. Heine, Fichte, Goethe, Brothers Grimm, Schiller, Hegel) encouraged the growth of a German consciousness.
- Post-1815 nationalist feelings first expressed in universities – growth of Burschenschaften.
- 'The Watch on the Rhine' – patriotic song based in Rhine Crisis of 1840.

Analysis/argument points could include:

Economic factors

- Industrial growth led to demands for a more united trading area within Germany and a removal of obstacles to trade and economic growth.
- Prussia saw opportunity for further growth but needed to remove trade barriers to allow for expansion.
- The economic isolation of Austria was a sign of things to come politically.
- Zollverein was called the 'mighty lever' of German unification and became a 'prototype' of later political unification as a Kleindeutsch model.
- Railway and road development spreading from Prussia caused other states to see Prussia as leader.
- Economic cooperation between German states became a model of later political development and helped to encourage nationalists to see that change was possible.

Political factors

- The ideas of the French Revolution inspired nationalists within Germany. Napoleon's Confederation of the Rhine had initially given some hope for unification.
- Nationalist feelings used by German princes to raise armies against Napoleon.

- Resentment of Metternich and Austria led to growth of national feeling.
- Political factors were of limited importance before 1850 because of Austrian control and repression.
- The fear of a common enemy (France) in 1840 once again increased patriotic unity against enemies.

Cultural factors
- Cultural identity created a feeling of common identity among German middle classes. This created 'seed bed' for future growth of nationalism.
- Students were an important factor in spread of nationalism as German education system meant students travelled between universities.
- Cultural factors were of limited importance before 1850 because of lack of literacy and the day-to-day concerns of a mainly rural population. Golo Mann wrote, 'Most Germans seldom looked up from the plough', meaning they had no real knowledge or care for cultural nationalism.

OVERALL

Overall, economic factors encouraged the separate German states to see that greater unity could have beneficial effects. In contrast, political and cultural national aims did not show such immediate benefits, so were less influential in the years before 1850.

---

5. To what extent was lack of popular support the main obstacle to German unification before 1850?

TOPIC AND TASK

The topic of this question is why there was a lack of movement towards German unity before 1850.

The task of this question is to:

1. Explain why the lack of popular support was an obstacle to German unification before 1850.
2. Explain other obstacles to German unification.
3. Reach a balanced conclusion that directly answers the question.

STRUCTURE
Context example

In 1800 there were around 400 separate states in what we now call Germany. When Napoleon invaded he reduced the number of states but he had no intention of uniting Germany. By 1815 Napoleon had been defeated and the former rulers of the German states returned to power with the intention of protecting the separate independence of the German states – with Austria's help.

> **TOP EXAM TIP**
>
> The context used here is the same as the context used for the previous German question (Q4). Remember, the context simply sets the scene and is not part of the answer to the question. Once you create one context for a specific topic, you can use it every time that topic comes up. Remember, it is the tasks that are different and the focus of your answer must be on what you are asked to do. It is **never** enough just to list historical facts.

Introduction points to signpost:
- Lack of popular support.
- The attitudes of the leaders of the German states.
- Austrian strength.
- Nationalists weak and divided.
- Attitudes of other foreign states.

THE DEVELOPMENT SECTION

To gain K marks you must include accurate and relevant factual detail, such as:

Lack of popular support
- Fichte's writings banned by Austria and failed to spread into the masses.
- Nationalist writers and composers, e.g. Brothers Grimm, Beethoven, Fichte, Goethe, Schiller, Hegel only had limited appeal – to those who could read and write or travel to attend concerts and plays.
- Burschenschaften, Hambacherfest and student demonstrations suppressed by Austria.

Divisions between states
- Germany divided into over 400 states in 1800.
- Northern German states were mostly Protestant and southern states mainly Catholic.
- Growing power of Prussia alienated some states, especially Catholic southern states.
- The Zollverein created an economic free-trade area.
- German Confederation set up in 1815.
- The leaders of the German states were opposed to unification, as they wanted to maintain their own power and privilege.
- During the Frankfurt Assembly King Frederick William abandoned the nationalists by refusing the crown of a united Germany.

Austrian strength
- The states within 'Germany' were all part of the old Holy Roman Empire, traditionally ruled by the Emperor of Austria.
- Austria dominated the German states after 1815.
- Treaty of Olmutz 1850 reasserted Austrian power over the German states.

Nationalists weak and divided
- Grossdeutsch and Kleindeutsch arguments divided opinion.
- Failure of the Frankfurt Parliament in 1849 caused by lack of army, lack of clear aims and lack of decisive leadership.

Attitudes of other foreign states
- Britain, France, Austrian Empire and Russia all had concerns.
- Fear of strong Germany dominating main trade route of Rhine.
- Fear about rise of strong central European power.
- Fear of new ideas of liberalism and nationalism spreading out across autocratic empires.

Analysis/argument points could include:
- Most 'Germans' felt greater identity to local areas, communities and their own states.
- Most Germans had little desire to see a united Germany.
- The mass of the population was apathetic and indifferent to politics and nationalist ideas.
- Austrian repression and censorship kept states divided.
- None of the Great Powers wanted to see the creation of a strong Germany that might upset the balance of power.
- Article 2 of German Confederation was geared towards guarding the separateness of individual states.
- Metternich opposed liberalism and nationalism and used force, censorship and spies to block any moves towards unity.
- The attitudes of other foreign states were an obstacle. The Congress of Troppau was a huge blow to nationalists within the German states. Liberal or nationalist uprisings that would threaten the absolute power of monarchs were to be suppressed.
- The Zollverein became a prototype of later political unification as a Kleindeutsch model. However, did states join the Zollverein just for financial gain and not necessarily hoping for political unity? Did the Zollverein prove an obstacle to political unity by scaring smaller states with the power of Prussia?

OVERALL
Overall, the main obstacle to unity before 1850 was Austria's desire to stop the spread of nationalism and liberalism. Associated with Austria were the ambitions of the German princes, many of whom tried to turn the clock back and stop new ideas spreading.

---

6. 'Without Adolf Hitler the Nazis would never have achieved power in Germany.' How valid is that opinion about the importance of Hitler's leadership to the rise of the Nazis by 1933?

TOPIC AND TASK
The topic of this question is the rise of the Nazis in Germany between 1919 and 1933.

The task of this question is to:
1. Explain how important the leadership of Hitler was to the Nazis up until 1933.
2. Explain other factors that helped the Nazis rise to power.
3. Reach a balanced conclusion that directly answers the question.

TOP EXAM TIP

This is one of two very different questions about the Nazis. To answer this question you must be able to write about the Nazis **before** 1933, in other words, how and why the Nazis rose to power in Germany. This is **not** about Nazi Germany **after** 1933. That is a very different question.

STRUCTURE

Context example
After the Great War ended Germany was ruled by a democratically elected government until 1933. However, between 1918 and 1933 there were many pressures on the new republic, some of which helped the Nazis rise to power.

Introduction points to signpost:
- The leadership and appeal of Adolf Hitler.
- The appeal of the Nazis.
- Anger over Treaty of Versailles.
- Economic crises.
- Weak Weimar democracy.

- Political plotting of Weimar leaders.
- Possible opposition was divided.

THE DEVELOPMENT SECTION
To gain K marks you must include accurate and relevant factual detail, such as:

Role of Adolf Hitler
- Hitler's attacks on Versailles attracted many Germans.
- He spoke of the 'stab in the back' by 'November criminals'.
- Hitler blamed Jews for Germany's problems.
- Hitler reorganised the party into an electoral campaigning machine after his release from prison in 1925.
- Hitler also saw importance of propaganda – he made alliance with Hugenberg.
- Hitler's political strength and focus manipulated Weimar politicians, such as von Papen and von Schleicher and even Hindenburg.
- Hitler developed policies that would appeal in some way to everyone.

Other factors
Weakness of the Weimar Republic
- Too much power in hands of president – article 48.
- PR voting system difficult to understand and led to coalition governments.
- Weimar government seemed weak when faced with demands to sign Treaty of Versailles and economic crises of 1923 and 1929.
- 'A Republic nobody wanted' – lack of popular support for the new form of government after 1918.

Attraction of Nazis
- Uniforms, drums, flags created illusion of strength.
- Publicity from November Putsch.
- Strong aggressive stance against communists.
- Image of patriotic defenders of Germany.
- Attractive to young.

Divisions among opponents
- Left split over treatment of Spartacists by Ebert and SPD in 1919.
- Political intrigue involving supposed democratic politicians – roles of von Schleicher and von Papen.

Economic problems
- Hyperinflation in 1923 had severe effects on the middle classes.
- The Great Depression of 1929 – Germany's dependence on American loans led to rising unemployment.
- Propaganda posters with slogans 'Only Hitler' and 'Hitler our only hope'.
- The depression polarised politics in Germany.

Analysis/argument marks could include:

Role of Adolf Hitler
- Hitler's speeches expressed how many felt about the difficulties of the 1920s and therefore attracted support to the party.
- Hitler gave Germans an excuse for losing the Great War and his promises of restoring pride and destroying Versailles attracted support.
- Hitler provided a scapegoat – the Jews – and allowed Germans to feel better about themselves.
- Hitler's reorganisation of Nazi party allowed it to capitalise on Germany's post-1929 problems.
- Hitler projected an image as the saviour of the Germans from communist threat.
- Hitler's use of propaganda allowed the Nazi Party to benefit from widespread publicity in newspapers and cinemas.
- Hitler's use of Weimar politicians undermined democracy from within and prepared way for dictatorship.

Other factors
Weakness of the Weimar Republic
- Weimar electoral system allowed Nazis a foothold in Reichstag – they could then appear credible and respectable.
- The Nazis appeared decisive and united in contrast to successive coalition governments.
- Many blamed government for letting Germany down, for example, by allowing French invasion. Nazis appeared to be 'more patriotic'.
- Nazi policies and strategy appealed to older, more traditional German values.

Divisions among opponents
- The lack of cooperation between socialist groups made any electoral opposition impossible. By splitting the 'left' vote Nazis won many seats.
- The plotting and intrigue of democratic politicians not only undermined faith in democracy but also gave Hitler respectability and influence.

Economic problems
- Hyperinflation in 1923 and then rising unemployment from 1929 scared the middle classes. The 1923 crisis was 'the scar that never healed'.
- A. J. P. Taylor wrote: 'It was the Great Depression that put the wind in Hitler's sails.' Propaganda posters with slogans 'Only Hitler' and 'Hitler our only hope' appealed to many who wanted direct and simplistic solutions.
- Hitler's claim that only Nazis could save Germany from the communist threat was attractive to middle classes who feared the communists.

OVERALL
Overall, Hitler was an opportunist who used developments in inter-war Germany to his advantage. He was like a buckle that held the Nazi belt together and without him the Nazi party would have gone nowhere. However, in terms of the Nazi rise to power, Hitler benefited from economic crises, political instability and a discontented population looking for answers to their problems.

USA 1918–1968

7. To what extent was fear of crime the main reason why attitudes towards immigrants changed in the early 1920s?

TOPIC AND TASK
The topic of this question is attitudes towards immigrants coming into America in the early 1920s.

The task of this question is to:
1. Explain why fear of crime caused attitudes to change.
2. Explain other reasons why attitudes changed.
3. Reach a balanced conclusion that directly answers the question.

STRUCTURE
Context example
In the early 20th century the USA had an open door for immigrants and by 1920 millions of immigrants had arrived in the USA. However, in the early 1920s America began to close its doors to immigration.

Introduction points to signpost:
- Fear of crime.
- The Red Scare.
- Pressure on housing and jobs.
- Nativism and small-town values.
- Racism and changes in the pattern of immigration.
- New laws restricting immigration.

THE DEVELOPMENT SECTION
To gain K marks you must include accurate and relevant factual detail, such as:

Fear of crime
- High crime rates in cities. Growth of ethnic-based gangs.
- The arrest and trial of Italian-Americans Sacco and Vanzetti.
- Organised crime, especially Mafia, involved in supplying illegal alcohol during prohibition.
- Mafia originated in Sicily, Italy. Famous gangsters such as Al Capone.

Other factors
The effect of World War One
- Many Americans supported isolationism. They wanted to keep out of foreign problems and concentrate solely on America.
- Many German immigrants living in the USA during World War One had sympathies for their mother country.

The threat to jobs
- Trades unions were trying to win better working conditions and wages. In the 1919 strikes, new immigrants were used as 'strike breakers'.
- New assembly line production methods only needed workers to do repetitive, unskilled jobs. Immigrants provided ready supply of cheap labour.

The Red Scare
- Wave of bombings and strikes in 1919 increased fears.
- Palmer raids and arrests reinforced public fears of immigrant revolutionaries.

- The 'Wobblies' – industrial workers of the world wanted revolution and became involved in some strikes and violent action.

Threats to housing supply in and around New York
- Growth of ethnically exclusive areas of cities, e.g. Little Italy, Little Poland.
- Supply and demand – with demand growing for low-rent housing landlords could increase rents without improving their property.

Small-town values and nativism
- Older, more established 'WASP' type immigrants worried about 'new' immigrants who were coming mainly from southern and eastern Europe – mostly Catholic, Jewish and those with different political beliefs, possibly revolutionary.
- Nativists saw immigrants as inferior people and a threat to traditional values.
- The KKK reinvented as an anti-immigrant organisation appealing to 100% Americanism.

Immigration restriction laws
- Pre-1920s restriction on Asian/Far Eastern immigration.
- Details of Quota Acts of 1920s.

Analysis/argument points could include:

Fear of crime
- High crime rates, growth of ethnic-based gangs led to feeling that immigrants were responsible for crime in cities.
- The arrest and trial of Italian-Americans Sacco and Vanzetti fed the stereotype that immigrants were responsible for crime.
- Mafia and famous gangsters such as Al Capone linked crime with immigrants in the public mind.

Other factors
The effect of World War One
- The post-war wave of immigration seemed to be bringing Europe's problems to America so resentment grew.
- Many immigrants from Germany and central and eastern Europe were seen as unpatriotic.

The threat to jobs
- Immigrants thought to be a threat to jobs; the use of immigrant labour as strike breakers caused huge resentment and an increase in the desire to stop immigrants coming into the country.

The Red Scare
- Wave of bombings and strikes in 1919 increased fears – belief they were caused by immigrant revolutionary groups.
- Palmer raids reinforced public fears of immigrant revolutionaries. 'Reds under the bed.'

Threats to housing in and around New York
- Growth of ethnically exclusive areas of cities increased suspicion of those who were different and maintained their differences once they arrived in America. Poor quality but expensive housing blamed on immigrants.

Small-town values and nativism
- Nativists and small-town Americans had big political influence and campaigned to restrict immigration in 1920s.

OVERALL
Overall, fear of crime was an important reason in turning public opinion against immigrants and preparing the way for legislation to limit immigration. However, the fear of crime was only part of wider fears about housing, jobs, political and social change that all combined into a fear of new influences in America.

> 8. To what extent was the overproduction of goods by American manufacturers the main reason for the depression of the 1930s?

TOPIC AND TASK
The topic of this question is why the USA suffered an economic depression in the 1930s.

The task of this question is to:
1. Explain why there was overproduction of goods by American manufacturers in the years before the depression began.
2. Explain why overproduction would cause economic problems.
3. Explain what other reasons caused the USA to suffer from a depression in the 1930s.
4. Reach a balanced conclusion that directly answers the question.

STRUCTURE
Context example
The 1920s are often called the 'Boom Years' in the USA. It seemed as if everyone was making money. The Republican government believed in laissez-faire policies that did not interfere with the economy. However, below the surface, there were problems that were to lead to economic collapse.

Introduction points to signpost:
- Overproduction of goods.
- Underconsumption.
- International economic problems.
- Government policy.
- Weakness of the US banking system.
- Wall Street Crash.

THE DEVELOPMENT SECTION
To gain K marks you must include accurate and relevant factual detail, such as:

Overproduction of goods
- More goods were being made than there were customers ready to buy them.
- New mass-production methods and mechanisation meant that production of consumer goods had expanded enormously.
- Cars, radios and other electrical goods had flooded the market.

Other factors
Underconsumption
- Almost 50% of the US population was poor – the bottom 40% of the population received only 12·5% of the nation's wealth.
- The top 5% of population owned 33% of the nation's wealth.
- Much production was left stockpiled, unsold.

International economic problems
- Results of World War One – many European countries could not afford to buy from America.
- Many European countries in debt to America.
- All European states, except Britain, placed tariffs on imported goods.

Government policy
- Throughout the 1920s, business had benefited from low-tax policies.
- Republican government policy of laissez-faire.
- US protectionist policy stopped foreign imports, e.g. Fordney McCumber tariff.
- Government policy meant no help for economy when it started to decline.
- Failure to help groups in USA, such as farmers, who did not benefit from the 1920s boom.
- Low capital gains tax encouraged share speculation which resulted in the Wall Street Crash.

Weakness of the US banking system
- Major problem was lack of regulation.
- Banking system was made up of hundreds of small, state-based banks.
- When one bank collapsed it often led to a run on other banks, resulting in a banking collapse and national financial crisis.
- Artificial boom in share prices boosted by bank lending.

Wall Street Crash
- Share buying became a popular gamble for many Americans who felt they could not lose. Money was borrowed to invest (buying on the margin).
- When shares began to lose value speculators rushed to sell, leading to collapse in prices.

Analysis/argument points could include:

Overproduction of goods
- By 1929 the market was saturated – those who could afford consumer goods had already bought them and there were no more customers to soak up production. Those groups who did not benefit from the boom and were therefore poor could not help the economy by buying expensive consumer goods.

Other factors
Underconsumption
- Producers depended on selling what they produced. Many Americans could not afford new consumer goods. The wealthy who did buy new consumer goods only amounted to a small percentage of US population.
- Underconsumption meant that demand did not keep up with production so factories shut down, leading to economic slow-down and then depression.

Government policy
- US policy of restricting foreign imports to protect American industry simply caused European countries to stop buying from USA.

Weakness of the US banking system
- Banking weakness – credit was too easy to get, but buying on hire purchase meant that if payments could not be kept up then the item bought was repossessed. That item was then returned to the producer and just added to unsold surplus stock.

Wall Street Crash
- Stock market crash did play a role in the depression but its significance was as a trigger, not a cause.
- The artificial boom in stocks and shares led many people to invest money they could not afford to risk.
- Collapse in confidence was a major reason for the depression.

OVERALL
Overall, overproduction of goods was one reason for the economic collapse in America after 1929 but, before it can be considered a main reason, other factors such as over-confidence, the Republican Party's economic policies and the assumption that the domestic market could keep on growing must also be weighed in the balance.

9. 'The Double V Campaign and the experience of World War Two marked the beginning of serious demands for civil rights in America.' How accurate is that statement about the growth of the civil rights campaigns after 1945?

TOPIC AND TASK
The topic of this question is the civil rights movement in the USA after World War Two.

The task of this question is to:
- Explain what the Double V Campaign was.
- Explain how important the Double V Campaign was in the development of the civil rights campaigns of the 1950s and 1960s.
- Describe and explain other reasons for the growth of the civil rights campaign.
- Reach a balanced conclusion that directly answers the question.

STRUCTURE
Context example
Before World War Two civil rights campaigns in the USA had made little progress. When the US army went to war in 1942 the armed forces were still segregated. The irony of segregated soldiers fighting to defeat Nazi racism was not lost on black soldiers who joined the Double V Campaign.

Introduction points to signpost:
- Action during World War Two to improve civil rights.
- Double V Campaign – US army segregated during World War Two yet black troops fighting against Nazi racism.
- Campaigns of A. Philip Randolph during World War Two.
- The impact of mass media in spreading awareness of continuing racial discrimination.
- Legal challenges and changes in civil rights.
- Growth of civil rights organisations.
- Effective civil rights campaigns.

THE DEVELOPMENT SECTION
To gain K marks you must include accurate and relevant factual detail, such as:

Double V and World War Two
- Black soldiers served in a segregated army and were often ignored in war reporting.
- Black soldiers spoke of the 'Double V Campaign': victory in the war and victory for civil rights at home.
- A. Philip Randolph highlighted the problems faced by black Americans during World War Two.
- March on Washington and Roosevelt's Executive order 8802.
- Fair Employment Practices Committee to investigate incidents of discrimination.
- The creation of the Congress of Racial Equality (CORE) 1942.

Other factors
Increasing awareness of continuing racial discrimination
- The spread of television and news reporting of civil rights cases increased pressure for change, e.g. murder of Emmet Till.
- Continuing Jim Crow laws provided a focus for growing campaigns.

Legal challenges led to change
- In 1954 *Brown* v. *Board of Education of Topeka* led to Supreme Court decision to end separate but equal decision of 1896.

Publicity and leadership
- Any significant protest events, such as the bus boycott or little Rock, that are used to demonstrate use of media and are not mentioned elsewhere would gain credit for K.

Effective black organisations formed

• 1957 Martin Luther King and other black clergy formed the Southern Christian Leadership Conference (SCLC) to coordinate the work of civil rights groups.

• Groups of black and white college students organised Student Non-violent Coordinating Committee (SNCC) to help the civil rights movement.

• Groups from SCLC, CORE and National Association for the Advancement of Colored People (NAACP) were involved in staged sit-ins, boycotts, marches and freedom rides.

The emergence of effective black leaders

• Martin Luther King
• Malcolm X
• Stokely Carmichael

Federal support

• Little Rock and use of federal troops.
• Kennedy's reaction to Birmingham campaign and response of authorities.
• Civil Rights Act.
• Voting Rights Act.

Analysis/argument points could include:

Double V and World War Two

• Black soldiers were fighting against Nazi racism to gain freedom, democracy and human rights yet black American soldiers had none of these back in USA.

• Resentment grew within the Black community as a result of the sacrifices made by Black servicemen who died fighting for America in World War Two.

• March on Washington and Roosevelt's response – Executive Order 8802 – showed how effective united and organised black campaigns could be.

• The creation of CORE was important in showing the growth in willingness to organise and campaign more effectively after the war.

Other factors

Increasing awareness of continuing racial discrimination

• Television and news reporting of civil rights cases increased pressure for change and motivated many to campaign for civil rights.

Legal challenges led to change

• Although the *Brown* v. *Board of Education of Topeka* decision only applied to education, it provided hope that things could change.

Publicity and leadership

• The Montgomery Bus Boycott (1955) and events at Little Rock Central High School (1957) provided inspiration to protestors that change could be achieved. They also demonstrated the importance of media coverage, leadership and support – King at Montgomery and federal support at Little Rock.

Effective black organisations formed

• Combined efforts of the civil rights groups gained publicity and led to end of discrimination in many public places.

The emergence of effective black leaders

• They were charismatic people who gave a public face to the movement and a focus for support.

Federal support

• Federal support was very important. Without it, laws would not have been changed or enforced.

OVERALL

Overall, the Double V Campaign and the experience of World War Two did mark a beginning in a renewed campaign for civil rights. Returning black servicemen saw how they had helped defeat Nazi racism in Europe yet faced prejudice and discrimination at home. As a result of those experiences, combined with the Supreme Court decision of 1954, there was an increasing belief that change was now possible. That motivational belief led on to the successful campaigns of the 1950s and 1960s.

Appeasement and the Road to War, to 1939

10. To what extent were aggressive fascist foreign policies caused by economic difficulties in the 1930s?

TOPIC AND TASK

The topic of this question is the reasons why fascist powers used aggressive foreign policies in the 1930s.

The task of this question is to:

1. Explain the extent to which economic problems caused fascist powers such as Germany and Italy to use more aggressive foreign policies in the 1930s.

2. To explain the other reasons why fascist powers adopted more aggressive foreign policies.

3. To reach a balanced conclusion that directly answers the question.

> **TOP EXAM TIP**
>
> In this appeasement section, where there are references in a question to fascist foreign policies or fascist powers, you must refer to both Germany and Italy. It is not enough just to deal with just one of those countries.

STRUCTURE

Context example

In the years after World War One new political ideologies took root in Europe: one of these was fascism. By the 1930s fascist foreign policy had become much more aggressive and expansionist and threatened the peace of Europe.

Introduction points to signpost:

* Economic difficulties in Italy and Germany.
* Fascist ideology demanded expansion and aggression in contrast to weak democracies.
* Resentment and desire to change Paris Peace Conference arrangements.
* Imperial ambitions of Italy; Lebensraum ambitions of Germany.

THE DEVELOPMENT SECTION

To gain K marks you must include accurate and relevant factual detail, such as:

Economic difficulties as a cause for fascist aggression

* Germany's and Italy's post-WW1 economic difficulties.
* Fascist economic policies in Italy in the 1920s – relative recovery.
* The impact of the world economic crisis 1929–1932 on the German and Italian economies intensified international competition and protectionism.
* Continuing economic problems in the 1930s.
* Propaganda advantages of expansionism.

Other factors

Legacy of World War One

* German resentment of war guilt, reparations, disarmament, lost territory.
* Italian resentment of failure to gain control of Adriatic. Italian desire to control Mediterranean – its Mare Nostrum.

Imperialism

* Mussolini's 'Roman' ambitions in the Mediterranean and Africa; Hitler's ambitions in eastern Europe and Russia.

Ideology

* Fascist hatred of communism and contempt for democracy.
* Hitler's aim to absorb all German speakers within 'Greater Germany'.

Leadership

* Personalities of Mussolini and Hitler and their style of leadership.

Weakness of the League of Nations

* Example of success of Japan in Manchuria in defiance of League of Nations.
* No League enforcement powers.
* Not a league of all nations.
* Seen as a victors' club to enforce unfair terms of 1919 settlements.

Analysis/argument points could include:

Economic difficulties as a cause for fascist aggression

* Germany and Italy's post-WW1 economic difficulties led political leaders to seek distractions for a population that might blame fascism for economic failure.
* Hitler knew that resources would be needed if Germany were to fight another war. He knew the lack of resources had led to German defeat in 1918.
* Mussolini wanted and needed prestige projects for his political stability.
* Most of the resources required by Mussolini and Hitler could only be gained by taking from some other place.

- Propaganda advantages – the need to keep the populations of Germany and Italy contented and believing fascist foreign policy worked in recovering former greatness and, in Germany's case, gaining revenge.
- Continuing economic problems in the 1930s and the need for additional resources, leading to aggressive, expansionist foreign policies, e.g. Italy in Abyssinia, German drive to the east (Lebensraum).
- Japan's attack on Manchuria had demonstrated how economic needs could be met by aggression.

Other factors
Legacy of World War One
- Both Germany and Italy left feeling resentful of peace treaties at end of war. Hitler and Mussolini staked political credibility on breaking those treaties and gaining revenge, therefore aggression needed.

Imperialism
- Both Hitler and Mussolini wanted the status and power of new empires involving conquest and demonstration of fascist superiority. That led to aggressive solutions.

Ideology
- Fascist ideology required conflict with democracy and communism and ultimate victory over them. Hence aggression to demonstrate comparative weakness and strength.

Leadership
- Both Hitler and Mussolini posed in military uniforms and wanted to appear strong, dominant alpha males. Conflict seemed inevitable in their desire for status and authority.

Weakness of the League of Nations
- Self-interest more important to Britain and France than League membership.
- Appeasement by and self-interest of Britain and France gave 'green light' to fascist powers to push for more. With each success they had, it became harder to stop them.
- Japanese attack on Manchuria demonstrated weak response of League, Britain and France.
- Examples of Italian invasion of Abyssinia, German Anschluss with Austria, the pressure upon and takeover of Czechoslovakia and the threat to Poland were all progressive escalation when it seemed no action would be taken to protect small states or to take action against aggression.

OVERALL
Overall, economic difficulties propelled fascist dictatorships into aggressive foreign policies, but at the root of those policies lay an ideology based on expansionism and racial superiority to justify that expansionism. Fascist states needed success to demonstrate superiority, and aggressive foreign policies in some ways helped to disguise the effects of economic difficulties.

---

11. To what extent was Britain's adoption of a policy of appeasement between 1936 and 1938 due to pressure from public opinion?

TOPIC AND TASK
The topic of this question is why Britain chose a policy of appeasement in the 1930s.

The task of this question is to:
1. Explain why public opinion was an important concern of government in the 1930s.
2. Describe the main concerns of public opinion in the 1930s in terms of appeasement and a reviving Germany.
3. Explain the other reasons why government used a policy of appeasement in the later 1930s.
4. Reach a balanced conclusion that directly answers the question.

> **TOP EXAM TIP**
>
> Always be aware of dates within a question. This question assesses issue 3 in the syllabus and the time period of any essay about this issue will always be 1936 to 1938, in other words, from the remilitarisation of the Rhineland until Anschluss. Both events should be referred to in your answer.

STRUCTURE
Context example
In 1918 the British public believed that 'the war to end all wars' had been fought and the League of Nations would keep the peace. However, by the 1930s, as the danger of war approached once again, Britain adopted appeasement as a means of avoiding another war.

Introduction points to signpost:
- Varied reasons for the policy of appeasement.
- Fear of bombing.
- Attitudes towards Germany.

- Military weakness.
- Fear of communism.
- Concern about Empire.
- Character of Prime Minister.
- Lack of allies.

THE DEVELOPMENT SECTION

To gain K marks you must include accurate and relevant factual detail, such as:

Appeasement in action
- Examples of appeasement during this time: references to remilitarisation of the Rhineland, non-intervention in the Spanish Civil War, Anschluss.

Public opinion was strongly anti-war
- The war to end all wars had been fought. Public opposed to another war.
- 1935 Peace Ballot, Oxford Union debate and Fulham by-election all evidence of anti-war attitudes.
- People worried about new technology that put Britain in front line. 'The bomber will always get through.'
- Fear of gas bombing reinforced by the movie *Things to Come*.

Other factors
Military weakness
- Run-down state of armed forces following WW1.
- Army: conscription ended after WW1, army scaled right down in size.
- Navy: not so run-down but not fully maintained and many obsolete ships.
- Air Force: lack of adequate air defences.
- Fear of a 'Three-front War'.

Economic difficulties
- Britain experiencing high unemployment and depression.

Lack of reliable allies
- Failure of League of Nations, e.g. Manchuria, Abyssinia.
- French political divisions, military weakness and Maginot mentality.
- US isolationism.
- Relative weakness of new eastern European states.

Concern about Empire
- Threats to Far East, India and Middle East/Suez Canal. British troops tied down in Palestine, India and other hot spots.
- Doubts over commitment of Empire and the Dominions in event of war, especially after Hertzog (PM South Africa) speech 1937.

Prime Minister Chamberlain
- Chamberlain believed Hitler would moderate views in power and be reasonable.
- He believed Hitler had to be negotiated with since he could not be 'wished away'.
- He had self-belief that he could deal with the European crises of 1938–39.

Fear of communism
- Nazi Germany seen as a buffer against communist spread.

Analysis/argument points could include:

Appeasement in action
- By 1936 the treaty arrangements had already been changed many times so was the remilitarisation really worth fighting over since it was German territory anyway?
- Non-intervention in Spain was a practical response. The civil war was not Britain's problem, and privately a Franco victory would help British investment interests in Spain.
- With Anschluss, once again it was not Britain's problem and there was a common feeling that Austrians were almost Germans anyway.

Public opinion was strongly anti-war
- Public hoped League would help and were opposed to rearmament.
- 1919 Peace Settlement was seen as too harsh on Germany and there was sympathy for what many saw as Germany's genuine grievances.

Other factors
Military weakness
- Exaggerated assessments of German military strength meant Britain wanted to avoid/prevent war.

Economic difficulties

- As Chamberlain had been Chancellor of the Exchequer he knew the cost of rearmament. His preference was social policy and in light of government spending cuts, appeasement was a cheaper option.

Lack of reliable allies

- Without support Britain could not hope to win a war so it was thought better to appease.

Concern about Empire

- Warnings of Chiefs of Staff and Chief of Imperial Defence that Britain could not win a simultaneous war with Japan in the east, Italy in the Mediterranean and North Africa and Germany in central Europe.
- Empire was biggest British concern, therefore Britain wanted to avoid war in Europe that would leave the Empire exposed to attack from Japan or Italy or rising nationalist campaigns, e.g. Arab revolt in Palestine.
- Britain needed to keep the Empire united and policed so did not want distractions in Europe. The warning of South Africa PM Hertzog in 1937 that SA would not fight with Britain to help Czechoslovakia alarmed Chamberlain.

Prime Minister Chamberlain

- Chamberlain had self-belief that he could deal with the European crises of 1938–39. Given Chamberlain's attitudes and his influence with the owners of certain newspapers and newsreels, did he follow public opinion, reflect it or create it?

Fear of communism

- A common belief was 'better Hitlerism than communism', so appeasement was a preferred option.

OVERALL

Overall, public opinion was important in helping the British government to maintain a policy of appeasement but did not lead the government to adopt the policy. Many reasons persuaded the government to adopt the policy, only one of which was the public's refusal to consider another war and their fear of what a future war might bring. In this sense, the government's adoption of the policy of appeasement was a happy marriage between government necessities and public wishes.

12. 'Munich was a triumph for British policy, not a failure.' How far can that view be supported?

TOPIC AND TASK

The topic of this question is the agreement reached between Hitler and Chamberlain at Munich in late September 1938.

The task of this question is to:

1. Explain why some people think that the Munich agreement was a defeat for Chamberlain and the British policy of appeasement.

2. Explain the reasons why the Munich agreement could be argued to be a success for Chamberlain and British policy.

3. Reach a balanced conclusion that directly answers the question.

STRUCTURE

Context example

After Anschluss in March 1938 it was clear that Hitler's next target would be Czechoslovakia. As war fears increased and two previous meetings between Chamberlain and Hitler had failed to settle the Sudeten issue, a third meeting was arranged at Munich.

Introduction points to signpost:

- British and French concerns about threats to Sudetenland.
- The Munich agreement.
- Reactions to Munich at the time.
- Criticism of Munich as failure.
- Changing attitudes about Munich as a success for British policy.

THE DEVELOPMENT SECTION

To gain K marks you must include accurate and relevant factual detail, such as:

- Sudetenland created by Paris Peace settlement out of Austro-Hungarian Empire – not part of Germany.
- Czechoslovakia was a successful example of multi-ethnic democracy.
- Czechoslovakian defences were strong but had been outflanked following the Anschluss.
- Konrad Henlein and Sudeten German Party – Hitler's instruction to Henlein to 'always demand more and never be satisfied'.
- Hitler's provocative speech 12 September 1938 – the Sudeten Germans are not defenceless.
- Britain and France were unprepared both in terms of military preparation and public opinion in support of action.

- Britain and France were not in a position to prevent German attack on Czechoslovakia in terms of:
  - geography – difficulties of getting assistance to Czechoslovakia;
  - public opinion – reluctant to risk war over mainly German-speaking Sudetenland.
- There was no prospect of any help from League of Nations or USA.
- Chamberlain's flights to Berchtesgaden and Bad Godesberg.
- Doubts about the willingness of some of British Empire and Dominions to support Britain in the event of war – Hertzog (PM South Africa) said his country would not help Britain in event of war over Czechoslovakia.
- Poland and Hungary were willing to benefit from the carve-up of Czechoslovakia.

Analysis/argument points for and against the view that Munich was a failure of British policy could include:

Munich a success?
- The agreement was an acceptance of the geo-political reality of the time after Anschluss.
- Hitler himself was dissatisfied by Munich. He had wanted war to boost his prestige so any frustration of his ambition was a success.
- There was no realistic hope of victory against any German attack.
- The agreement provided time to prepare for future conflict, especially air defences.
- There were serious doubts about the willingness of some of the British Empire and Dominions to support Britain in the event of war. By avoiding war, the unity of the Empire was preserved.
- What is the point of taking moral stand against aggression if it results in defeat?
- When war with Germany did come Britain could not be blamed, having done all it could to avoid confrontation.

Munich a defeat?
- Czech defences, major industrial centres and transport links all lost at Munich.
- Czech resources became Nazi assets further tilting balance of power against Britain.
- Hitler given what he wanted in Sudetenland.
- British policy a humiliating surrender to Hitler's threats and another abandonment of the Paris Peace settlements.
- A betrayal of Czechoslovakia and democracy. In March 1936 Britain had promised to help France oppose any future threat to Czechoslovakia.
- Czechoslovakia was left wide open to further German aggression.
- Hitler's ambitions in eastern Europe were encouraged by British climb-down at Munich.
- Further alienation of Soviet Union leading eventually to Nazi-Soviet pact.
- Poland left vulnerable.
- Impact on public opinion and hopes for peaceful settlement of Czech problem were dashed by Nazi invasion of Bohemia and Moravia in March 1939.
- Czech crisis lead directly to British promise to help Poland.
- Hitler was dissatisfied by Munich. He had wanted war to boost his prestige. He felt he could gain from a small, successful war over Poland. When the Polish Corridor crisis arose Hitler said, 'This time no bastard is going to stop me.'

OVERALL
Overall, the Munich agreement was a recognition of the inevitable. To some it represented a sell-out of principle and friends, to others it was a sensible solution to a problem that really was not Britain's problem. For Britain, peace was preserved for a time and as there was no real reason for, or practical possibility of, fighting, the Munich settlement was the realistic outcome of a difficult situation.

Answers to Practice Exam A, Paper 2

The Wars of Independence, 1286–1328

1. How fully does Source A illustrate the issues that arose as a result of the succession problem in Scotland 1286–1292?

   Use the source and recalled knowledge.   10

This is a 10-mark question.

There are up to 4 marks for selecting four relevant parts of the source's content and:

- explaining why these selections are relevant in terms of the question;
- using some recall to support and develop the points in the source.

Four relevant selections from the source are:

- Edward saw a way of expanding his influence over Scotland.
- The threat of civil war in Scotland.

- The simmering issue of overlordship.
- The Guardians intended the Treaty of Birgham to keep Scotland separate and free from control by England.

TOP EXAM TIP

Do **not** just list the four points from the source and leave it. You must explain why they are relevant to answering the question.

Recall to support your selections could include:

- Death of Alexander III and unclear succession.
- The granddaughter of Alexander III, Margaret Maid of Norway, was the lawful heiress – Margaret and the Norwegian connection.
- Appointment of Guardians by nobles and Church.
- Conditions attached by Guardians to Treaty of Birgham.
- William Fraser's letter to Edward and possibility of civil war.
- Edward I's aim to establish feudal overlordship across the Scottish kingdom.
- Edward I, king of England, perhaps had the intention of joining Scotland to England.

There are up to 7 marks for using relevant and accurate recall that shows a wider knowledge of the issues and links to the question, such as:

- Death of Alexander's first wife, Margaret, and all of his children.
- Yolande, Alexander's second wife, provided no male heir.
- The role of the Guardians.
- Community of the Realm required the agreement of barons, nobles and the Church.
- Long-term ill feeling between the Comyn and Bruce families.
- Claims could only be settled by use of family tree linking back to birthright from David I.
- The Guardians compromised the independence of their kingdom by inviting Edward's mediation.
- The Competitors and their claims.
- The Great Cause, the process of Norham and the decision at Norham.
- Edward's decision in favour of Balliol.
- Edward's demand for homage.

---

2. How far does Source B explain the reasons for Edward's subjugation of the Scots in 1296?

   Use the source and recalled knowledge.   **10**

This is a 10-mark question.

There are up to 4 marks for selecting four relevant parts of the source's content and:

- explaining why these selections are relevant in terms of the question;
- using some recall to support and develop the points in the source.

Four relevant selections from the source are:

- While we still owed him fealty and homage we made an alliance with the king of France against him.
- We have defied our lord the king of England and have withdrawn ourselves from his homage and fealty by renouncing our homage.
- We have sent our men into his land of England to burn, loot, murder and commit other wrongs.
- We have fortified the land of Scotland against him.

TOP EXAM TIP

Do **not** just list the four points from the source and leave it. You must explain why they are relevant to answering the question.

Recall to support your selections could include:

- Edward demanded feudal military forces from Scotland to go to war against Philip IV of France in 1294.
- The Guardians signed a treaty with France in John's name.
- Feudal system of land-ownership, homage and fealty.
- Overlordship and the responsibility to obey feudal superior.
- Scots invasion of northern England and attacks on Carlisle.
- As overlord Edward should have access to Scottish castles. They were his property.

There are up to 7 marks for using relevant and accurate recall that shows a wider knowledge of the issues and links to the question, such as:

- Edward's invasion of Scotland:
  - his massacre of Berwick's inhabitants;
  - battle of Dunbar;
  - Edward's march northwards;
  - capture of Balliol.
- Humiliation of Balliol – Toom Tabard.

- Balliol made to renounce Treaty of Alliance with France.
- Scotland was stripped of 'identity' as independent nation – Stone of Destiny, records of Scottish Crown, Scottish taxation all to London.

---

3. How useful is Source C in showing the importance of William Wallace to Scottish resistance against the English?

In reaching a conclusion you should refer to:

- *the origin and possible purpose of the source;*
- *the content of the source;*
- *recalled knowledge.*

5

This is a 5-mark question.

There are up to 2 marks for showing that you have <u>understood</u> the importance of the origin and the purpose of the source.

TOP EXAM TIP

You must explain why the origin and purpose make the source useful for revealing information relevant to the question.

Origin:
- A letter from Wallace and Murray as joint Guardians to the merchants of Lübeck.
- This is one of very few primary sources from Wallace and illustrates his use of diplomacy in helping Scotland to recover after invasion and defeat by England 1296–1297.

Possible purpose:
- To assert the independence of Scotland but more practically to persuade important trading ports in northern Germany (the Hanseatic League) that Scotland was once again open for business after invasion by the English and their destruction of traders' property in Berwick.
- Scotland needed to build up reserves of its strength if it was to survive against English threats.

There are up to 2 marks for selecting three relevant parts of the source's content and:
- explaining why these selections are relevant in terms of the question;
- using some recall to support and develop the points in the source.

Three relevant selections from the source are:
- Andrew of Moray and William Wallace, leaders of the army of the kingdom of Scotland.
- ... asking to have it announced to your merchants that they can have safe access to all ports of the Scottish Kingdom with their merchandise.
- ... the Kingdom of Scotland, thanks be to God, has been recovered by war from the power of the English.

TOP EXAM TIP

Do **not** just list the three points from the source and leave it. You must explain why they are relevant to answering the question.

Recall to support your selections could include:
- Wallace and Murray's victory at Stirling Bridge.
- Wallace and Murray made joint Guardians of Scotland.
- Wallace and Murray accepting and supporting the king in exile, John Balliol.
- The importance of trade in metals and manufactured goods to the Scottish economy and war effort.
- The European trade connections with Scotland.

There are up to 2 marks for using relevant and accurate recall that shows a wider knowledge of the issues and links to the question, such as:
- Edward's invasion of Scotland 1296.
- Edward's destruction of Berwick, especially the Red Hall warehouse of Flemish merchants and the property of other European merchants.
- Edward's attempts to take away Scotland's national identity.
- Edward's attempt to turn Scotland into a province of England.
- Wallace's resistance a part of a wider rising against Edward's administration in Scotland.
- Wallace's murder of Sheriff of Lanark.
- Murray's rising in the north of Scotland.

---

4. To what extent do Sources D and E agree in their opinions about why the Scots won the Battle of Bannockburn?

Compare the sources overall and in detail.

5

The comparison question is worth 5 marks.

You must start your answer by making an OVERALL COMPARISON. There are up to 2 marks for making an overall comparison. An overall comparison of the sources should include:

- Overall the sources disagree in their views about why the Scots won at Bannockburn.
- Source D believes the planning, preparation and tactics of the Scots explains their victory whereas Source E lays the blame for defeat squarely on the failures of English leadership, planning and tactics.

You must continue your answer by comparing the sources IN DETAIL.

There are up to 4 marks for finding four different sets of comparison points within the sources.

> **TOP EXAM TIP**
> It is not enough just to quote a sentence from one source, then compare by quoting from the other. You must also explain the point being made by your extracts in your own words and use some recall to develop your comparison. That is what is meant by a developed comparison.

In detail:

1. The main disagreement between the sources is over whether the Scots won the battle or the English, by their actions, lost the battle.
    - Source D states, 'The Scots won at Bannockburn because of careful planning.'
    - On the other hand, Source E claims that, 'the Battle of Bannockburn was not so much won by the Scots as lost by the English.'
2. The sources disagree that the Scots won because of effective use of terrain.
    - Source D claims that 'Scottish control over the high road to Stirling was vital for victory and before the battle the Scots dug potts in and around the road to force the English to look for other ways to reach the castle.'
    - On the other hand, Source E believes that it was English failure to use terrain effectively that led to their defeat. The author argues, 'The English army was well equipped with scouts who knew the terrain well so why then did Edward's forces march onto boggy land?'
3. The sources disagree about the importance of the Scots schiltrons to the victory at Bannockburn.
    - Source D argues the schiltrons were very important and states, 'The Scottish schiltrons were mobile and were used to attack as well as defend. By keeping the schiltrons pushing forward the Scots gave the English no room to move or to regroup.'
    - On the other hand, Source E thinks it was the English failure to deal with schiltrons that led to their defeat. He argues, 'Why had they learned nothing … They knew that the way to deal with schiltrons was to … send wave after wave of arrows into the packed masses of Scots.'
4. The sources disagree over the importance of Bruce in winning the battle.
    - Source D believes that Bruce was an inspiring leader and claims his leadership was very important to success and states, 'Bruce's leadership was vital. He is credited with using the "small folk" to charge at a crucial moment of the battle, thereby demoralising the English.'
    - On the other hand, Source E thinks the English lost because Edward II's leadership was so poor. He writes, 'King Edward II lacked his father's skill and … the English chain of command was still unclear.'

In conclusion, the main difference between the sources is that Source D believes it was a victory fully deserved by the Scots whereas Source E thinks the Scottish victory was really the result of English mistakes.

The Treaty of Union, 1689–1740

> 1. How far does Source A explain incidents leading to worsening relations with England?
> *Use the source and recalled knowledge.*
> 10

This is a 10-mark question.

There are up to 4 marks for selecting four relevant parts of the source's content and:

- explaining why these selections are relevant in terms of the question;
- using some recall to support and develop the points in the source.

Four relevant selections from the source are:

- The effects of a century of neglect and discrimination.
- Many asked how a country could succeed when its own Head of State actively opposed its interests.
- Concern over William's possible involvement in the Glencoe massacre.
- In 1701, the English Parliament, without consultation with Scotland, passed the Act of Settlement.

> **TOP EXAM TIP**
> Do **not** just list the four points from the source and leave it. You must explain why they are relevant to answering the question.

Recall to support your selections could include:
- Under the Union of the Crowns, Scottish interests were relegated beneath those of England.
- Impossible for Scots to have their own foreign policy if it opposed that of England.
- Differences between Scottish and English interpretations of the Revolution of 1688–89.
- Articles of Grievances of 1689 by Scottish Parliament.
- Glencoe Massacre and William's role in this.
- Continued Jacobite support in some parts of Scotland.
- Conflict of interest – monarch tended to sacrifice Scottish interests to those of England.
- William's use of political management to control the Scottish Parliament.
- Collapse of the Darien Scheme and William's part in its collapse.
- Problems surrounding the succession due to Queen Anne being without an heir.
- Scots afraid of losing legal and religious identity under Hanoverian rule.
- England concerned at possible threat from Scotland if the Stuarts were restored.
- The Scots were angered because they were not consulted but were just expected to accept the Hanoverian succession.

There are up to 7 marks for using relevant and accurate recall that shows a wider knowledge of the issues and links to the question, such as:
- In 1701, the English passed the Act of Settlement. This established the Hanoverian succession.
- The Scots were angered at not being consulted which resulted in a series of anti-English Acts being passed.
- Increased patriotic feeling.
- Feeling that Scotland was being overlooked – provincial relegation.
- Queen Anne had made it clear that she considered herself 'entirely English'.
- Scotland was brought into the War of the Spanish Succession.
- Response to this was the Act Anent Peace and War.
- Act of Security was rejected by the Queen as 'unreasonable'.
- Act of Security said Scotland might not choose the same monarch on the death of Queen Anne.
- In the future, the Scottish Parliament would decide on any involvement of Scotland in wars.
- Evidence of support for the exiled Stuart dynasty.
- English ministers, e.g. Godolphin, were allowed to interfere in Scottish affairs.
- February 1705, Alien Act put pressure on the Scots.
- Tension heightened with the *Worcester* incident.
- Scots angered at being drawn into the war with France without consultation.
- English resentment at continued Scottish trade with France.
- Additional tension arising from English Episcopalian opposition to Presbyterian Church in Scotland.

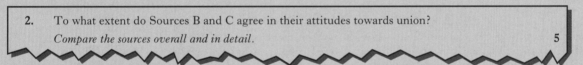

2. To what extent do Sources B and C agree in their attitudes towards union?
   Compare the sources overall and in detail.

   5

The comparison question is worth 5 marks.

You must start your answer by making an OVERALL COMPARISON. There are up to 2 marks for making an overall comparison. An overall comparison of the sources should include:
- Overall the sources disagree about the effects of union; Source B argues that union will benefit Scotland while Source C believes union will hurt Scotland.
- A further development of the overall comparison could suggest that Source B states that Scotland will benefit in several practical ways from union whereas Source C's main objection is that Scotland will lose its independence and freedoms.

You must continue your answer by comparing the sources IN DETAIL.

There are up to 4 marks for finding four different sets of comparison points within the sources.

TOP EXAM TIP

It is not enough just to quote a sentence from one source, then compare by quoting from another. You must explain the point being made by your extracts in your own words and use some recall to develop your comparison. That is what is meant by a developed comparison.

In detail:
1. The sources disagree about the effect of the union on the Scottish (Protestant) Presbyterian religion.
   - Source B believes that union will guarantee 'security for our religion' as 'the kingdom of England is a Protestant kingdom'.
   - Source C argues that union will 'ruin ... our religion'.
2. The sources disagree about the benefits of union to future trade.
   - Source B thinks that Scotland will benefit from trade opportunities opened up by the union. It states, 'England has trade and other advantages to give us'.
   - On the other hand, Source C believes that Scotland cannot rely on benefiting economically. It states, 'the English ... may if they please discourage the most valuable branches of our trade'.

3. Sources B and C also disagree over the political freedoms that may have been won or lost by union.
   - Source B argues that union would guarantee political freedom in Scotland and states, 'England has freedom and liberty, and joining with them was the best way to secure that to us'.
   - On the other hand, Source C believes that union with England will, 'ruin ... our laws and liberties. As a result ... Our parliament and all that is dear to us will be extinguished.'
4. Finally, the sources disagree about the independence and safety of the country.
   - Source B believes that union would help protect both Scotland and England and states, 'I saw no other method for securing peace, the two kingdoms being in the same island.'
   - On the other hand, C believes that England has simply taken over Scotland and in a way defeated it. It states, 'As a result, one of the most ancient nations so long and so gloriously defended will be suppressed.'

In conclusion, the sources disagree completely, B arguing for the benefits of union and C arguing that union will hurt Scotland in many ways.

TOP EXAM TIP

You do not have to end with a short conclusion that directly answers the question asked but it will impress the examiner!

---

3. How useful is Source D as evidence of the methods used to pass the Treaty of Union?

   In reaching a conclusion you should refer to:
   - *the origin and possible purpose of the source;*
   - *the content of the source;*
   - *recalled knowledge.*

   5

There are 5 marks for this question.

There are up to 2 marks for showing that you have <u>understood</u> the importance of the origin and the purpose of the source.

TOP EXAM TIP

You must explain why the origin and purpose make the source useful in terms of the question.

Origin:
- Written by Lockhart of Carnwath who had been appointed a Commissioner for arranging the union with England. He was therefore in a position to report the methods used to pass the union.
- Lockhart was anti-union and his sympathies were with the Jacobites; a year before his memoirs were published he had taken part in an attempt to repeal the union.

Possible purpose:
- Lockhart alleged extensive use of bribery of Scottish MPs prior to the Treaty of Union and published a list of bribes paid by the English Treasury. The purpose of this extract from his memoirs is to give his biased viewpoint concerning the passing of the union.
- This memoir supports his allegations that opposition to the union was soon removed by bribes, financial or otherwise.

There are up to 2 marks for selecting three relevant parts of the source's content and:
- explaining why these selections are relevant in terms of the question;
- using some recall to support and develop the points in the source.

Three relevant selections from the source are:
- The ministers were concerned about the government of the Kirk ... But no sooner did Parliament pass an act for the security of the Kirk than ... many of them changed their tune and preached in favour of it.
- But the truth of the matter lies here: a sum of money was necessary to be distributed amongst the Scots.
- And this distribution of it amongst the proprietors of the Company of Scotland was the best way of bribing a nation.

TOP EXAM TIP

Do **not** just list the three points from the source and leave it. You must explain why they are useful in answering the question.

Recall to support your selections could include:
- Scottish Presbyterian worries about role of English Church.
- Presbyterians were against the use of bishops in the Church.
- Presbyterians wanted the Church to look after itself by means of its own kind of parliament called a General Assembly.
- Presbyterians did not want any interference from the king.

- The Kirk had opposed the union until the passing of the Act of Security.
- Scotland was paid compensation called the Equivalent.
- The Equivalent totalled nearly 400 000 pounds, about £26 million in today's money.
- Scotland paid less tax for the first seven years.
- Darien disaster had almost bankrupted Scotland.
- Equivalent paid to compensate many who had lost fortunes with Darien failure.
- Members of the Squadrone Volante, the group that changed sides in the union debate, received money from the Equivalent.
- Duke of Queensberry received 20 000 pounds – more than £2·5 million in today's money.
- Critics of the union say that Queensberry was building up a fund of money that he would use to bribe other Scottish politicians.
- Duke of Argyll of the Court Party was given a military promotion, became a Lord and was given money with a value today of £1·3 million.

> **TOP EXAM TIP**
>
> Never just include information because you think it is about the topic of the question. You must always link it to answering the question by writing something like: 'This information helps to explain the usefulness of the source because ...'

There are up to 2 marks for using relevant and accurate recall that shows a wider knowledge of the issues and links to the question, such as:

- Trade was a major incentive for the union.
- The union would end the Navigation Acts, which excluded the Scots from trade with the English Colonies.
- The Act of Security for the Kirk guaranteed that it would remain Presbyterian.
- Opposition from the Kirk melted away.
- Many welcomed the compensation for the Darien losses.
- Troops were placed along the border in 1706 – perhaps it was better to accept a negotiated union rather than a forced one.
- The opposition was far from united.
- Hamilton's role as the leader of the opposition.
- Guarantees were made for the retention of Scottish institutions, e.g. legal system and Convention of Royal Burghs.

> **4.** How fully does Source E summarise feelings in Scotland about the effects of the union up to 1740?
>
> *Use the source and recalled knowledge.* **10**

This is a 10-mark question.

There are up to 4 marks for selecting four relevant parts of the source's content and:

- explaining why these selections are relevant in terms of the question;
- using some recall to support and develop the points in the source.

Four relevant selections from the source are:

- The Jacobites, rightly enough from their standpoint, saw it as a deadly blow to the hopes of the exiled Stuarts.
- The Episcopalians, most of whom favoured the Stuarts, were afraid that the union would secure Presbyterianism.
- The Presbyterians welcomed the Protestant succession but feared that, under the union, bishops would again be thrust upon the Church of Scotland.
- The merchants of Scotland feared they would be swamped by English trade. They did not believe the union offered entry to 'the shelter of an empire'.

> **TOP EXAM TIP**
>
> Do **not** just list the four points from the source and leave it. You must explain why they are relevant to answering the question.

Recall to support your selections could include:

- Jacobites had become the focus for anti-union sentiment after the union was passed.
- Jacobites wanted to reverse the Revolution of 1688–1689 and restore the Stuart dynasty.
- Jacobites said that they would end the union if the Stuarts were restored.
- Episcopalians feared domination by the Presbyterian Church of Scotland.
- Episcopalians were numerically smaller and seen as a minority, alien Church by many.
- Episcopalians torn between support for Anglican Church and support for Jacobite cause.
- Anglican Prayer Book allowed to be used in Episcopalian services.
- 1710 High Church Tories attempted to remove privileges of Church of Scotland.
- The Kirk was unhappy with the Toleration and Patronage Acts of 1712.
- Patronage Act gave Scottish nobles the right to appoint ministers in their parishes, thereby offending Presbyterian practice.

- Union resulted in increased taxes and duties. It was difficult for some industries to cope with English competition.
- Trade with France was lost.
- Tobacco industry developed in Glasgow, but still not developed by 1740. Scottish linen industry suffered in relation to English wool industry.

> **TOP EXAM TIP**
>
> Use the word **partly!** By saying you agree partly, or a source explains something partly, you have the opportunity to explain what the points made in the source mean. You can then write something like, 'On the other hand' and then bring in lots of recall to suggest things that are relevant to the question but were not mentioned in the source. By doing this you will be able to demonstrate your own recalled knowledge and you will also have a balanced answer that answers a 'How fully?' question.

There are up to 7 marks for using relevant and accurate recall that shows a wider knowledge of the issues and links to the question, such as:
- The majority of Scots were discontented with the union at this time.
- Scottish peers who gained English peerages were not getting to sit in the House of Lords.
- The government introduced stricter English treason laws, an early example of infringement of the treaty.
- Other measures passed by the Westminster parliament infringed the Treaty of Union, e.g. Patronage Act and no rotation of sittings between Edinburgh and London, and this led to disillusionment with England and the union.
- Many Scottish industries, e.g. wool and paper, had suffered from English competition.
- Others who had supported the union turned against it, such as Seafield who tried to have the union repealed in 1713.
- Short-term economic dislocation resulting in unemployment.
- Porteous Riot of 1736 in Edinburgh can be linked to disillusionment with the union.
- Smuggling became more widespread in Scotland after the union.
- Protests against introduction of the Malt Tax.
- Economic benefits of union had failed to materialise.
- Trade with Europe, particularly with Holland, had declined.
- 1711 Greenshields case, overruling the Scottish law courts.
- In the years immediately after 1707, the economic disadvantages severely outweighed the advantages; only by 1740 were the benefits becoming apparent.
- Only a small number of Scots engaged successfully with the colonies.
- Investment and distribution of Equivalent welcomed by some.
- Improvements in agriculture, fisheries and manufacture gained more support for union by 1740.

Scotland and the Impact of the Great War, 1914–1928

> 1. How far does Source A show the experience of Scots on the Western Front?
>   *Use the source and recalled knowledge.*
>   10

This is a 10-mark question.
There are up to 4 marks for selecting four relevant parts of the source's content and:
- explaining why these selections are relevant in terms of the question;
- using some recall to support and develop the points in the source.

Four relevant selections from the source are:
- Our artillery were bombarding the German trenches night and day, smashing up the barbed wire.
- Then it was over the top and the best of luck. Men were … blown to pieces lying mangled in shell holes.
- We were held up by machine gun fire and had to try and dig ourselves in with our entrenching tools.
- Only about 50 returned out of the 500 that advanced.

> **TOP EXAM TIP**
>
> Do **not** just list the four points from the source and leave it. You must explain why they are relevant to answering the question.

Recall to support your selections could include:
- Experience of fighting and its effects: bombardment, over the top, machine guns, etc.
- Loos was first taste of action for Kitchener's New Army volunteers.
- Scottish losses were dreadful and no part of Scotland was unaffected.
- One-third of British casualties at Loos were Scottish.
- Experience of trench warfare: Scots units suffered the same hardships as others – rats, lack of sanitation, etc.
- Dangers of trench warfare: shelling, gas, etc.

There are up to 7 marks for using relevant and accurate recall that shows a wider knowledge of the issues and links to the question, such as:
- High Scottish casualty rate – proportionately the highest of any combatant country in war caused by fighting.

- Experience of Scots in trenches: conditions such as trench foot, rats, etc.
- Battle of Arras in 1917 – forty-four Scottish battalions and seven Scottish-named Canadian battalions attacked on the first day, making it the largest concentration of Scots to have fought together. One third of the 159 000 British casualties were Scottish.
- Scots involvement in other battles, such as Somme, Cambrai and Third Ypres.
- Fifty-one Scottish infantry battalions took part in the Somme offensive at some time.
- No mention of Scottish women, e.g. Scottish nurses working behind front line. Others served with armies of other nations, e.g. Mairi Chisholm serving with Belgian army. Also, the Scottish Ambulance Unit.
- No mention of Scots in leadership. Douglas Haig, an Edinburgh-born Scot, was made Commander-in-Chief by 1915.

TOP EXAM TIP

The 'How far?' question asks about only part of an issue so remember to keep your recalled knowledge relevant to the question.

---

2. How useful is Source B as evidence of attitudes about recruitment and the Defence of the Realm Act?

   In reaching a conclusion you should refer to:
   - *the origin and possible purpose of the source;*
   - *the content of the source;*
   - *recalled knowledge.*   5

This is a 5-mark question.

There are up to 2 marks for showing that you have <u>understood</u> the importance of the origin and the purpose of the source.

TOP EXAM TIP

You must explain why the origin and purpose make the source useful in terms of the question.

Origin:
- Report of Maclean's trial in *Forward*, a socialist newspaper, so it was likely to be sympathetic towards Maclean.
- Mainstream newspapers of the day considered protest against war unpatriotic and condemned Maclean for weakening the war effort.

Possible purpose:
- By reporting Maclean's trial, the report also managed to put forward socialist arguments against the war and in particular against joining up to fight.

There are up to 2 marks for selecting three relevant parts of the source's content and:
- explaining why these selections are useful in terms of the question;
- using some recall to support and develop the points in the source.

Three relevant selections from the source are:
- Maclean explained that he had been a socialist for 15 years and he condemned all armies as part of the international arms race.
- Maclean may have undermined support for recruitment by claiming that soldiers were no better than murderers.
- The Sheriff (judge) explained that DORA (Defence of the Realm Act) was an exceptional law passed to protect national security.

TOP EXAM TIP

Do **not** just list the three points from the source and leave it. You must explain why they are useful to answering the question.

Recall to support your selections could include:
- Many socialists opposed the war.
- Social Democratic Party, Independent Labour Party and Socialist Labour Party had been intensely anti-war and anti-militarist before the war.
- Socialists split over the issue but revolutionary agitators, under Maclean's leadership, were increasing in number.
- Socialists argued that war only benefited the capitalist class. The armies were filled with working-class men who gained nothing from war.
- Majority supported war, either for patriotic reasons or as the result of propaganda.
- Recruitment had been very high, although declining by February 1915.
- Many saw socialist opposition as unpatriotic.

- DORA was passed within days of outbreak of war to protect against anything that might be a threat to national security.
- Speeches such as Maclean's were judged a danger to security as such speeches undermined support for the war effort and recruitment in particular.

There are up to 2 marks for using relevant and accurate recall that shows a wider knowledge of the issues and links to the question, such as:
- Socialists split over whether or not to support the war.
- The Labour Party joined the wartime coalition in 1916. The ILP did not.
- Many saw Maclean as a great Scottish revolutionary. Although he was inspirational to many he was only ever on the edge of Scottish political developments during the war. He was a broken figure partly because of his many arrests and treatment in prison.
- The radicalisation of Scottish politics, e.g. Red Clydeside.
- Socialist opposition grew when conscription was introduced in 1916.
- However, most workers supported the war and worked hard.

TOP EXAM TIP

Never just include information because you think it is about the topic of the question. You must always link it to answering the question by writing something like: 'This information helps to explain the usefulness of the source because ...'

---

3. To what extent do Sources C and D agree about post-war emigration from Scotland?

   Compare the sources overall and in detail.

   5

The comparison question is worth 5 marks.

You must start your answer by making an OVERALL COMPARISON. There are up to 2 marks for making an overall comparison. An overall comparison of the sources should include:
- Both sources are contemporary accounts of emigration from the Hebrides in the 1920s.
- They agree on how emigration was arranged and also on the emigrants' destination, the assistance given by the Canadian government and motives for migration.

You must continue your answer by comparing the sources IN DETAIL.

There are up to 4 marks for finding four different sets of comparison points within the sources.

TOP EXAM TIP

It is not enough just to quote a sentence from one source, then compare by quoting from another. You must also explain the point being made by your extracts in your own words and use some recall to develop your comparison. That is what is meant by a developed comparison.

In detail:
1. The sources agree about the areas the emigrants left.
   - Source C reported, 'Thirty families ... are leaving Benbecula, South Uist and Barra.'
   - Source D also mentions that, 'crofting families ... have gone out from Barra and South Uist.'
2. The sources agree that the emigration was organised or at least encouraged by priests in the Catholic Church.
   - Source C states that: 'This scheme was initiated by the Rev. Father McDonnell.'
   - Source D also reports 'the readiness on the parts of some priests to consider emigration'.
3. The sources agree on the destination of the emigrants and on the assistance given to them.
   - Source C mentions that the emigrants, 'are going out with the encouragement of the government of Ontario, Canada.'
   - Source D describes how 'The Canadian government is apparently willing to do its part ... at the expense of the Canadian government'.
4. The sources also agree on the reasons for emigration. They both mention the push factors of poverty and lack of work.
   - Source C describes the migrants as, 'many ... going out to seek employment in Canada or take up work on the land'.
   - Source D also claims that push reasons were the main reason for migration by stating that most emigrants were 'escaping unemployment and destitution at home'.

In conclusion, the sources agree about post-war emigration, identifying poverty and unemployment as major factors in persuading people to leave Scotland.

TOP EXAM TIP

You do not have to end with a short conclusion that directly answers the question asked but it will impress the examiner!

> **4.** How fully does Source E explain the impact of the war on political developments in Scotland?
> *Use the source and recalled knowledge.* **10**

This is a 10-mark question.

There are up to 4 marks for selecting four relevant parts of the source's content and:

- explaining why these selections are relevant in terms of the question;
- using some recall to support and develop the points in the source.

Four relevant selections from the source are:

- In the 1920s all three major parties actively supported the Union. Home Rule bills went nowhere.
- Lack of popular support for Labour Party's election manifesto promise to fight for restoration of the land of Scotland to the Scottish people.
- Scottish culture and Scottish identity seen by some as being eroded by the spread of Englishness in all aspects of life.
- Lack of support for new National Party of Scotland – its leaders gained less than 5% of the vote in each constituency.

TOP EXAM TIP

Do **not** just list the four points from the source and leave it. You must explain why they are relevant to answering the question.

Recall to support your selections could include:

- Labour support increased tenfold between 1910 and 1918.
- In 1922, 42% of Glasgow electors voted for Labour.
- Membership of the Independent Labour Party trebled during the war years.
- Mainstream popular newspapers all strongly pro-union.
- The Scottish Renaissance also had an effect on the Scottish independence movement and laid roots of the Scottish National Party. However, in the 1920s there was very little national support for separation.
- Radicalism after war: possible 'revolutionary spirit' immediately after the war but long-term triumph of gradualist approach (working for gradual change through parliament). Maclean had wanted revolution but others in ILP, such as Maxton, Kirkwood, Johnston and Wheatley, wanted slower change.
- Increasing support in some areas for nationalism – National Party of Scotland established in 1928, with leaders McCormick and Muirhead.
- Conservatives and Liberals gave no support to Scottish Home Rule.
- Post-war patriotic support for UK left little room for nationalist sympathies or support.

TOP EXAM TIP

Use the word **partly!** By saying you agree partly, or a source explains something partly, you have the opportunity to explain what the points made in the source mean. You can then write something like, 'On the other hand' and bring in lots of recall to suggest things that are relevant to the question but were not mentioned in the source. By doing this you will be able to demonstrate your own recalled knowledge and you will also have a balanced answer that answers a 'How fully?' question.

There are up to 7 marks for using relevant and accurate recall that shows a wider knowledge of the issues and links to the question, such as:

- At the end of the war, the Labour Party in Scotland was dominated by the ILP. By 1928, the ILP had lost influence.
- In the 1922 election Labour made the breakthrough as the second political party: 29 of their 142 seats were in Scotland.
- In the 1924 election Labour won 34 seats in Scotland. Labour formed a minority government, led by a Scot, Ramsay MacDonald, with Liberal support.
- Clydeside was the main centre of communist politics after the formation of the British Communist Party in 1920.
- Strengthening of Conservative Party especially after George Square riots and fears of revolution. Conservatives won 30% of the vote in 1918. In the second election of 1924 they won 38 seats in Scotland compared to Labour's 26.
- The Liberal Party was a split party and very much weakened.
- In the second 1924 election the Liberals won only 9 seats in Scotland.

TOP EXAM TIP

The 'How fully?' question asks about a whole issue so in this case any information about political changes in Scotland after the Great War could be used as long as it is presented in a way that is relevant to the question.

Britain 1851–1951

---

1. To what extent did Britain make progress towards democracy between the 1850s and 1918?

TOPIC AND TASK

The topic of this question is the growth of democracy in Britain between the 1850s and 1918.

The task of this question is to:

- Suggest as many things as possible that are necessary for a country to be called a democracy.
- Explain how far these things had been achieved in Britain by 1918.
- Argue that perhaps Britain was more democratic but not entirely a democracy by 1918 by suggesting other things that still had to be achieved.
- Reach a balanced conclusion that answers the question directly.

TOP EXAM TIP

This is one of two very different questions about democracy. To answer this question you must be able to explain **how** Britain became more democratic. It is **not** about **why** the changes happened. That is a different type of question.

STRUCTURE

Context example

In 1850 the vote was restricted to property owners and renters. Only one in six adult males could vote. By 1918, the vote had been extended to all males aged 21 or over and some women aged 30 or over. Clearly Britain was more democratic, but not entirely so.

Introduction points to signpost:

In a democracy certain things are necessary:

- The right to vote.
- A choice of who to vote for.
- Information about candidates in order to make an informed choice.
- A fair system of voting.
- A fair system of representing the people.
- Politicians to be accountable to the voters.

THE DEVELOPMENT SECTION

To gain K marks you must include accurate and relevant factual detail, such as:

- Giving the vote to more people in 1867, 1884 and 1918.
- Giving greater choice with the creation of the Labour Party in 1900.
- Providing the electorate with information. Detailed knowledge for this point should include: political parties became more nationally organised; the spread of basic education and public libraries; the growth of the railway network.
- Making the voting system fairer with the Secret Ballot Act 1872, Corrupt and Illegal Practices Act 1883 and the redistribution of seats in 1867, 1885 and 1918.
- Making the system more accountable to the electorate by reforming the House of Lords in 1911.
- The payment of MPs (1911).

Analysis/argument points to explain **how** the above factual detail helped Britain make progress towards democracy by 1918 could include:

- The right to vote is an essential ingredient in a democracy. In an election the adults of the country choose how they will be governed.
- In a democracy the voting system must be fair and people should be able to express their opinions without fear or bribery.
- People should be represented fairly so that each MP represents roughly the same number of people.
- Providing the electorate with information – the organisation of political parties ensured their 'messages' got across to electorate.
- The spread of basic education, public libraries and the growth of the railway network allowed news to spread, politicians to travel the country and an informed and participating electorate to develop.
- Until 1900 there was no party to represent the new working-class voters. The formation of the Labour Party helped fix that problem.
- People should not be excluded from the political system because they are poor. The payment of MPs (1911) allowed people of any background to consider participating directly in the political system.
- House of Lords was not elected but it did have the power to veto or block any laws being made by the elected House of Commons. Britain became more democratic when the House of Lords was reformed.

To **balance** your answer you could also explain in what ways Britain had not yet achieved full democracy.

- Only some women gained the vote in 1918. Male/female voting rights not made equal until 1928.
- Plural voting and university constituencies effectively gave some people two votes. These anomalies were not abolished until 1948.
- In 1949 the two-year delaying power of the House of Lords was reduced to only one year but the power of the unelected House of Lords in law-making still continues.
- The voting system in the UK is still First Past the Post with the result that votes for losing candidates are ignored and the winner takes all.
- 18 year olds not allowed to vote until 1969.

OVERALL

Overall, by 1918 Britain was much more democratic than it had been in 1850. The electorate was bigger, the electoral process was fairer and by 1918 the elected MPs represented the British people rather than the British land! However, some issues still remained to be sorted, not least of which was the issue of political equality for women.

> **2.** How far was concern over poverty the main reason for the Liberal government's decision to introduce social reforms between 1906 and 1914?

TOPIC AND TASK

The topic of this question is **why** the Liberal reforms happened.

The task of this question is to:

1. Explain why there was concern about poverty in the early twentieth century and how far that concern pushed the Liberals into passing social reforms.
2. Explain the other reasons why the Liberals introduced social reforms between 1906 and 1914.
3. Reach a balanced conclusion that directly answers the question.

> ### TOP EXAM TIP
> This essay is **not** about the Liberal reforms themselves! It is about **why** they happened. Do **not** get sidetracked into writing details of the reforms. It will waste time and gain you no marks.

STRUCTURE

Context example

Throughout most of the 19th century poverty was seen as a sign of personal failure. The beliefs of self-help and laissez-faire urged individuals to look after themselves, or, if all else failed, to enter poor houses for assistance. However, in 1906 the Liberals began a series of social reforms to help the poor. Why did they do this?

Introduction points to signpost:

- Booth and Rowntree reports on poverty.
- Worries about national security.
- Concerns over national efficiency.
- The Liberals saw political advantage in social reforms.
- New Liberal ideas about government help for the 'deserving poor' took root within government.
- Example of municipal socialism showed what could be done to help the poor.

THE DEVELOPMENT SECTION

To gain K marks you must include accurate and relevant factual detail, such as:

Concerns about poverty

- The reports of Charles Booth and Seebohm Rowntree in London and York.
- Levels of poverty around 30% exposed by the reports.
- Booth's poverty line, primary poverty and secondary poverty.
- Changing ideas of self-help, laissez-faire and the 'deserving poor'.

Concerns about national security

- 25% of the volunteers to fight in the Boer War were rejected because they were physically unfit to serve in the armed forces.

Concerns over national efficiency

- By the end of the 19th century British industry was facing serious competition from USA and Germany.
- Germany had started social reforms in the 1880s.
- Need for healthier workforce.

Political advantage

- Since 1884, many more working-class men had the vote and the Liberals had tended to attract many of those votes.
- In 1900 the Labour Representation Committee was formed (and became known as the Labour Party). This new party promised social reforms.
- Labour would take votes away from the Liberals and would damage Liberal chances of defeating the Conservatives in future elections.

New Liberalism
- New Liberal ideas became important when Prime Minister Campbell Bannerman died in 1908 AND 'New Liberals', such as Lloyd George and Winston Churchill, entered the Cabinet.
- New Liberals argued that only the national government had enough power to really make a difference to national poverty.

The example of municipal socialism
- Municipal socialism means that some towns and cities had Liberal local governments that used local taxes mainly paid by the wealthy to provide better services for the poor.
- Example of Joseph Chamberlain in Birmingham.

Analysis/argument points could include:

Concerns about poverty
- There was a growing acceptance that poverty was often beyond an individual's ability to escape from. That was an important factor in influencing the government that action must be taken to ease poverty.
- The reports of Charles Booth and Seebohm Rowntree shocked the government into action. They provided statistical facts about poverty that could not be ignored.
- People had not believed that poverty was so consistently high throughout the country.

Concerns about national security
- Fears about national security led to concerns about whether or not Britain could protect its interests in a future war against a bigger and stronger enemy.

Concerns over national efficiency
- Growing economic competition from abroad raised worries that poorly educated and poorly fed workers could not help Britain recover its position.
- Germany had introduced many social reforms, such as old age pensions and sickness benefit, so why could Britain not follow that example?

Political advantage
- Liberals worried that the new Labour Party might take votes away from Liberals. It was in Liberal interests to tempt voters away from Labour by carrying out social reforms.

New Liberalism
- They argued that the state (the government) should help the deserving poor to cope with problems over which the poor had no control.

The example of municipal socialism
- By the end of the century, Liberal politicians were arguing that what was being done locally in some cities should be organised by national government to help the poor everywhere in the nation.

OVERALL

Overall, concern over poverty was one reason why the Liberals were persuaded to pass their social reforms between 1906 and 1914. However, several other factors also played their part in persuading the Liberal government to take action. Perhaps the main reason was the growing realisation that the deserving poor – those who were poor through no fault of their own – could not simply use 'self help' to solve their difficulties.

3. To what extent did the Labour government of 1945–1951 deal successfully with the social problems facing Britain after World War Two?

TOPIC AND TASK

The topic of this question is the post-war social reforms of the Labour government between 1945 and 1951.

The task of this question is to:
1. Describe the social problems that faced Britain in 1945.
2. Explain how Labour tried to deal with each of the social problems.
3. Judge how effective each of the reforms was in helping deal with the social problems.
4. Reach a balanced answer that directly answers the question.

STRUCTURE

Context example

The Beveridge Report was published in 1942 and identified 'Five Giant' social problems facing Britain. The report became a bestseller for a population that hoped that 'post-war would be better than pre-war'. When Labour came to power in 1945, they based their reforms on attacking Beveridge's Five Giants.

Introduction points to signpost:
- Beveridge's Five Giants – want, squalor, ignorance, idleness and disease.
- What Labour did to tackle each of the Five Giants.
- The continuing debate on the effectiveness of Labour's reforms.

THE DEVELOPMENT SECTION

To gain K marks you must include accurate and relevant factual detail, such as:

Tackling want

- 1946 National Insurance Act – compulsory contributory scheme for every worker.
- Contributions paid for sickness and unemployment benefit and old age pensions.
- National Assistance Act for those not in work and paying no contributions to National Insurance.
- Family Allowance Act for second and subsequent children and the allowance paid directly to mothers.
- Industrial Injuries Act of 1946 – compensation for injuries at work paid for by the government to cover all workers.

Tackling disease

- The NHS entitled everybody to medical care free at point of use.
- The NHS was based on three main aims:
  - universal access: the NHS was for everybody. The old health system, based on insurance schemes, did not cover everyone;
  - comprehensive: the NHS would treat all medical problems;
  - free at point of use: no patient would be asked to pay for any treatment.
- In reality the service was, and still is, paid for by the National Insurance payments made by every worker, supplemented by general taxation.
- By 1950 charges were introduced for spectacles, prescriptions and dental treatment.

Tackling ignorance

- The Education Act of 1944 (1945 in Scotland) raised the school leaving age to 15 and all children were to get free secondary education.
- All children sat the 11+ exam.
- Results of exam decided the type of secondary school a child went to.
- Originally planned to have different levels of school:
  - in England, technical school, secondary modern and grammar school;
  - in Scotland, junior secondary and senior secondary.

Tackling squalor

- Many houses damaged in war.
- Labour promised to build 200 000 each year.
- Building materials shortage.
- 'Prefabs' intended as a stop-gap to meet overwhelming needs.
- Even in 1951 Labour still averaged well over 200 000 houses a year.
- The New Towns Act in 1946 laid the plans for 14 New Towns to be built.
- Town and Country Planning Act 1947.

Tackling idleness

- Labour's answer to the problem of unemployment was nationalisation.
- Labour believed they could control and manage the economy more effectively and maintain full employment.

Analysis/argument points could include:

Want

- Pension levels remained below basic subsistence levels.
- National Assistance provided a safety net through which no person should fall into serious poverty.
- Family Allowance paid directly to mothers, who it was felt were more likely to spend the money on what the children and the household needed.

Disease

- Illness and medical issues had been major causes of poverty. NHS was welcomed and did provide medical help 'from the cradle to the grave'.
- Concerns about cost of NHS and introduction of some charges led to resignation of some Labour ministers.

Ignorance

- For those who passed the 11+ exam or 'qualify' the system worked well. The thousands of children who failed it were trapped in a world of low expectations and inferior education.

Squalor

- By 1951 there was still a serious housing shortage and long waiting lists for council housing.
- There was criticism of 'soulless' council estates and destruction of old inner city communities.
- Many liked the new houses with separate bedrooms, indoor toilets, electricity and hot/cold running water.

Idleness

- Criticism that nationalisation led to inefficiency and losses in the nationalised industries.
- Failure to attract talented management.

OVERALL

Overall, Labour was successful in establishing a welfare state after 1945 and in so doing made serious attempts to tackle all of Beveridge's Five Giants. Although there is still doubt about how successful Labour was, there is no doubt that Labour's reforms did make significant improvements to the lives and opportunities of people in post-war Britain.

Germany 1815–1939

4. How accurate is it to claim that between 1815 and 1850 there was a real growth in German nationalism?

TOPIC AND TASK

The topic of this question is nationalist feeling in Germany between 1815 and 1850.

The task of this question is to:

1. Provide evidence that there was real growth in nationalist feeling in Germany between 1815 and 1850.
2. Show evidence that the growth of nationalist feeling in Germany was limited at this time.
3. Reach a balanced conclusion that directly answers the question.

STRUCTURE

Context example

In 1800 there were around 400 separate states in what we now call Germany. When Napoleon invaded he reduced the number of states but he had no intention of uniting Germany. By 1815 Napoleon had been defeated and the former rulers of the German states returned to power with the intention of protecting the separate independence of the German states – with Austria's help.

Introduction points to signpost:

- Economic development in Prussia and its influence on the growth of national awareness.
- Political developments, such as growing support for nationalism and liberalism.
- Cultural nationalism and growing awareness of German identity.
- Growing resentment of Austrian influence within Germany.
- The revolutions of 1848.
- Indications of lack of growth – suspicions of Prussia, Austrian opposition, political repression.

THE DEVELOPMENT SECTION

To gain K marks you must include accurate and relevant factual detail, such as:

Growth involving cultural nationalism

- Fichte's writings.
- Nationalist writers, thinkers and musicians, e.g. Brothers Grimm, Beethoven, Fichte, Goethe, Schiller, Hegel.
- Burschenschaften, Hambacherfest and student demonstrations.
- Events of 1840.

Growth involving economic nationalism

- Industrial growth in early nineteenth century and rise of middle class.
- Better transport links.
- Railway network.
- Prussia created customs union in 1818 that was to become the Zollverein.
- Prussian gains of territory in 1815.
- Economic isolation of Austria.

Growth involving political nationalism

- The ideas of the French Revolution.
- Nationalist opposition to foreign rule and growth of national awareness in years after 1815.
- Repressive actions of Metternich – Carlsbad Decrees and the Six Acts.
- Congress of Troppau – the decision taken by the representatives of Austria, Prussia and Russia.
- 1848 revolutions and the Frankfurt Parliament.
- Grossdeutsch/Kleindeutsch future for Germany.
- Frederick William of Prussia, Austria and Olmutz.

Analysis/argument points that both support and contradict the belief that there was a real growth in nationalist feeling could include:

- Growing German pride in cultural traditions. Fichte's writings emphasised German states united by language and shared cultural heritage. However, the impact of poets, musicians, writers was largely on educated Germans and not everyone was interested in such ideas. Most Germans were not aware of cultural developments – historian Golo Mann wrote, 'Most Germans seldom looked up from the plough.'
- Increasing nationalist tendencies of student societies and their impact as students travelled around the states as part of their studies. But very little was achieved and it was easily suppressed by 'old order' under Austrian guidance.
- The economic isolation of Austria was a sign of things to come politically.
- The focus of growth and economic influence shifted to North Sea trade area and the iron and coal resources of Prussia's new territory around the Rhineland.
- The Zollverein became a prototype of later political unification as a Kleindeutsch model. However, did states join Zollverein just for financial gain and not necessarily hoping for political unity?
- Main aim of the German Confederation was to maintain the independence of each individual state so this was not a move towards national unity.

- Growth in nationalism encouraged by political developments was very limited between 1820 and 1848.
- Political moves towards unity seriously hampered by Metternich and repression of liberal ideas by old rulers of German states.
- Metternich successful in suppressing nationalist growth – Carlsbad Decrees and the Six Acts.
- The Congress of Troppau was a huge blow to nationalists within the German states. Liberal or nationalist uprisings that would threaten the absolute power of monarchs were to be suppressed.
- Frankfurt Parliament was divided. As a result of Olmutz and the humiliation of Prussia, German nationalism seemed dead by 1850.

OVERALL

Overall, there was a growth in German nationalism between 1815 and 1850. Although political nationalism only grew slowly between 1815 and 1850 because of Austrian repression, cultural nationalism continued to encourage feelings of German-ness. However, it was economic nationalism that really took off with the Zollverein and showed the German states the personal benefits that could come from greater unity.

> **5.** 'Bismarck's leadership was vital to the creation of a united Germany by 1871.' How accurate is that opinion?

TOPIC AND TASK

The topic of this question is Bismarck and the unification of Germany.

The task of this question is to:

1. Explain the importance of Bismarck to the process of German unification.
2. Explain other factors that helped lead to German unification that may have helped Bismarck but were not the result of his own creations.
3. Reach a balanced conclusion that directly answers the question.

> **TOP EXAM TIP**
>
> Questions about Bismarck usually require you to look at other reasons for unification as well. You will never get a question that just asks you to write about his three wars of unification. Beware you do not get dragged into just telling the story of these wars.

STRUCTURE

Context example

Before Bismarck became Minister President of Germany, the German states remained divided and under Austrian influence. Earlier hopes for German unification had failed in 1849 and at Olmutz in 1850 it seemed that Prussian hopes to lead a united Germany had ended.

Introduction points to signpost:

- Bismarck's role as architect of German unification focused on:
  - foreign policy;
  - diplomacy;
  - opportunism.
- Other factors outwith Bismarck's power were leading towards unity such as:
  - Prussian military and economic power;
  - Austrian weakness.

THE DEVELOPMENT SECTION

To gain K marks you must include accurate and relevant factual detail, such as:

- Bismarck and Realpolitik/diplomacy in the three wars against Denmark, Austria and France.
- The issue of Schleswig-Holstein and war with Denmark.
- Bismarck's diplomatic moves with Austria before war. Austria isolated as Bismarck made arrangements with Russia, France and Italy.
- Treaty of Prague 1866.
- Hohenzollern candidature and Ems Telegram to provoke war with France.

Other factors

- Prussia a powerful state before Bismarck: economic power based on railway network and Zollverein allowed Bismarck to finance and equip army.
- Austrian power – politically, militarily and economically in decline well before Bismarck came to power.
- Prussian army reforms.

Analysis/argument points could include:

- Bismarck's main aim was to increase the power of Prussia rather than unite Germany.
- Bismarck made use of coincidental political developments and used them to his advantage, e.g. Schleswig-Holstein issue, Hohenzollern candidature.
- Bismarck very astute at manipulating events, e.g. Ems Telegram, his wisdom with lenient Treaty of Prague with Austria.

- Bismarck also in right place at right time – growing hopes for nationalism and an increased German national consciousness among the educated classes prepared the ground for Bismarck.
- The Bismarck debate: did he have a master plan? Was he simply lucky? Did his skill lie in the effective use of opportunities? He did not deal the cards but played his hand well.
- Bismarck an architect or master planner – or simply an opportunist?

Other factors
- Bismarck would not have been successful without a strong Prussian army. The economic base for its growth and the army reforms were not his work. They were tools used by Bismarck. Zollverein often credited as the 'mighty lever of German unification'.
- Bismarck was lucky – Austrian power was politically, militarily and economically in decline well before Bismarck came to power.
- One argument is that Bismarck did not really unite Germany but rather he Prussianised it by bringing other German states under the power and control of Prussia.

OVERALL

Overall, Bismarck was like a gardener who used his skills and experiences to create the garden of German unification. However, like any gardener, Bismarck needed to use tools that he personally did not create, such as the economic benefits of the Zollverein in creating a strong Prussia. Also, like a gardener who makes the best of good weather, Bismarck had used lucky opportunities that were beyond his control but nonetheless helped his overall purpose.

6. How far was the use of fear, force and threats responsible for the survival of the Nazi state between 1933 and 1939?

TOPIC AND TASK

The topic of this question is how the Nazis maintained power in Germany between 1933 and 1939.

The task of this question is to:
1. Explain how the Nazis used fear, force and threats to maintain control in Germany between 1933 and 1939.
2. Explain other reasons why the Nazi state retained control over Germany between 1933 and 1939.
3. Reach a balanced conclusion that directly answers the question.

TOP EXAM TIP

This is one of two **very different questions** about the Nazis. To answer this question you must be able to write about the Nazis **after** 1933, in other words how they kept control of Germany between 1933 and 1939. This is **not** about **how** the Nazis rose to power before 1933. That is a very different question.

STRUCTURE

Context example

In 1933 a legal revolution brought Adolf Hitler and the Nazis to power in Germany. The democratic republic of Weimar Germany ended and was replaced by a totalitarian dictatorship that lasted until the end of World War Two.

Introduction points to signpost:
- Use of fear/force/threats to maintain control.
- Weakness/divisions among opponents.
- Use of law/constitution to maintain control.
- Success of domestic policies in winning popular support.
- Success of foreign policy in winning popular support.

THE DEVELOPMENT SECTION

To gain K marks you must include accurate and relevant factual detail, such as:

Use of fear/force/threats
- Role of the Gestapo.
- Concentration camps set up.
- The use of the SS.
- Network of informants set up.
- Psychological pressure and fear.
- Persecution of minority groups within Germany.
- Arbitrary arrests meant everyone in fear that they too might become 'vanished people'.
- Use of exile and executions.

Other factors that help explain Nazi control over Germany:

Weakness/divisions among opponents
- Opponents arrested, killed or in exile.
- Opposition groups could not unite or have large-scale meetings.
- Lack of cooperation between socialists and communists going back to the Spartacist revolt.
- Those against the Nazis faced severe punishments and so did their families.

Use of the law and constitution

- Political parties outlawed.
- Anti-Nazi members of the civil service were dismissed.
- Nazis became lawmakers, law interpreters in courts and law enforcers. **No** legal check on Nazi power.
- Acts Hostile to the National Community (1935) – Nazis allowed to persecute opponents in a legal way.
- Opposition groups persecuted and ruthless treatment of opposition publicised.

Success of domestic policies

- Effective propaganda praised the improvements in Germany under the Nazis.
- Reduction in unemployment was very popular.
- Massive programme of public works also popular.
- Germany was given better living standards under Hitler.
- Göring's policy of 'guns before butter'.
- Creation of the *Volksgemeinschaft* (national community).
- Nazi youth and education policy.
- Nazi policy towards the Jews.
- Nazi family policy – Kinder, Küche, Kirche.
- Strength through Joy organisation.
- A Concordat with the Catholic Church was reached: Catholics accepted Nazi rule. A Reichsbishop was appointed as head of the Protestant Church.

Success of foreign policy

- Nazi success in foreign policy attracted support among Germans.
- Destruction of Treaty of Versailles.
- Restoration of pride.
- Nazis seemed to deliver what they promised – the taking away of the shame of 1919.

Analysis/argument points could include:

Use of fear/force/threats

- The use of secret police, informants and arbitrary arrest created a sense of social isolation and fear.
- With no one expressing opposition, it seemed as if everyone supported the Nazis.
- Being anti-Nazi was quickly linked to being unpatriotic.
- The majority seemed content to witness the persecution of unpopular minority groups.

Other factors that help explain Nazi control over Germany:

Weakness/divisions among opponents

- No effective united opposition meant the opponents of Nazism could not gain widespread public attention.
- Hitler benefited from the lack of cooperation between socialists and communists.
- Opponents were liable to severe penalties so fear was a significant reason for lack of opposition to Hitler and survival of the Nazi state.

Use of the law and constitution

- Checks and balances removed from the system. Nazi lawmakers were also judges in courts and law enforcers on the streets so there was no easy way to resist or oppose Nazis.
- Acts Hostile to the National Community (1935) – legal persecution of opponents created a feeling that opposition was pointless.
- After the Night of Long Knives, few people were prepared to raise voices against the state.

Success of domestic policies

- People accepted propaganda showing success of economic policies at the time. It all seemed so much better than the years of depression preceding the Nazis.
- Nazi social policies claimed as successes in propaganda. With no evidence to contrary, the German public accepted the 'truth' that the Nazi state was much better than Weimar democratic weakness. Hence Nazi state unchallenged and popular.
- As Nazi influence increased over all aspects of German life most people simply acquiesced in (just accepted) Nazi rule.

Success of foreign policy

- Nazi success in foreign policy satisfied a need for revenge and restored a sense of pride, in contrast to the Weimar years of resentment and feelings of injustice.

OVERALL

Overall, the Nazi state remained in control of Germany between 1933 and 1939 by careful use of carrot and stick methods. If Germany was a donkey, that German donkey was made to move the way the Nazis wanted by both forcing it and by offering it benefits to encourage a 'feel-good factor'. Positive improvements to the lives of most Germans led them to accept and even welcome Nazi rule. For those who opposed or objected to Nazi rule, fear and force and terror could easily be applied.

USA 1918–1968

7. How far was the Ku Klux Klan responsible for the lack of progress towards civil rights for black Americans in the years up to 1941?

TOPIC AND TASK

The topic of this question is the obstacles in the way of achieving civil rights for black people **before** 1941.

> **TOP EXAM TIP**
>
> When you see a date in a question always make sure you know if the question is asking about years **before** the date or **after** the date.

The task of this question is to:

1. Explain how and why the KKK was an obstacle on the path towards civil rights.

2. Explain other obstacles or difficulties that prevented black people from achieving civil rights before 1941.

3. Reach a balanced conclusion that directly answers the question.

STRUCTURE

Context example

Soon after slavery was abolished in the 1860s, the KKK was established as a threats organisation to keep freed slaves 'in their place'. By 1900, segregation and discrimination were strictly enforced in the southern states of the USA. There seemed to be almost no chance of making progress towards civil rights for black Americans.

Introduction points to signpost:

* The actions of the Ku Klux Klan.
* Racist attitudes, Jim Crow and the Supreme Court ruling of 1896.
* Black poverty in the South.
* Divided aims of the early civil rights organisations.
* The Great Migration north.
* Lack of federal support.

THE DEVELOPMENT SECTION

To gain K marks you must include accurate and relevant factual detail, such as:

The actions of the Ku Klux Klan

* KKK started in the 1860s to prevent former slaves achieving equal rights.
* Klan revival in 1915.
* Three million members in the 1920s, including police, judges and politicians.
* Secret organisation, difficult to campaign against.
* Motto in 1920s – '100% American'.
* Hiram Wesley Evans leader (Imperial Wizard) in 1920s.
* Klan use of violence – lynching and beatings.
* Klan created fear by their appearance – men in white robes, guns, torches, burning crosses.
* Klan had powerful political influence, especially in the South.

Other factors
Racist attitudes, Jim Crow and the Supreme Court ruling of 1896

* The South had been a slave-owning culture until the 1860s. Old habits die hard.
* In the South, a long-established racial hierarchy existed with whites on top and black people at the bottom of social ladder.
* Jim Crow laws created from 1870s used to discriminate against black people and to segregate.
* Supreme Court 'Separate but Equal' Decision of 1896 reinforced Jim Crow laws.
* Segregation became respectable and nationally accepted.

Lack of political influence

* Black men given right to vote by 15th Amendment but states found ways to impose voting restrictions, e.g. 1898 case of *Mississippi* v. *Williams* – voters must understand the American Constitution.
* Grandfather Clause created a barrier to black people voting.
* Federal government had little interest in civil rights.
* President Wilson was not opposed to segregation – 'Segregation is not humiliating and is a benefit for you black gentlemen'; he also introduced segregation in federal offices.
* President Roosevelt in 1930s refused to support anti-lynching legislation.

Black civil rights organisations split

* Booker T. Washington and Tuskegee Institute – black people should earn white respect by hard work and education before expecting civil rights.
* W. E. B. Du Bois founded the National Association for the Advancement of Colored People (NAACP) 1909 – a national organisation whose main aim was to oppose discrimination through legal action.
* Marcus Garvey – founded the UNIA (Universal Negro Improvement Association) which aimed to get blacks 'Back to Africa' and to make Africa 'the defender of Negroes the world over'.
* UNIA based mainly in New York.
* UNIA advocated separatism, 'Back to Africa' and Black Pride.

Discrimination and poverty in the north

- The Great Migration – Word War One created huge demand for workers in industrial north.
- No official segregation in north but life still difficult – black Americans still 'last hired, first fired'.
- Development of urban ghettos: crime, lack of education, racism still very common.
- Chicago riots 1919 and Tulsa riots of 1920s.
- Average black worker was unskilled and ill paid.
- Excluded from skilled work by trades unions and racially prejudiced employers.

Black poverty in the South

- Sharecropping kept most rural black Americans in debt trap.
- Most black people in the South did not own land and some states identified ownership of property as a voting qualification.

Analysis/argument points could include:

The actions of the Ku Klux Klan

- People too scared by Klan violence to organise or campaign for civil rights.
- Klan controlled all official routes of complaint.
- Klan influenced lawmakers and law enforcers.
- Klan prevented civil rights organisations growing, especially in South.

Other factors
Racist attitudes, Jim Crow and the Supreme Court ruling of 1896

- Black population saw little chance of change. Civil rights seemed to have no support from any official group.

Lack of political influence

- Roosevelt needed white southern Democrat support in US Congress to get his New Deal into action. Any help given to black civil rights would lose that white political support for Roosevelt.
- Since so few black people could vote easily, there was no political advantage in supporting civil rights.
- As so few black people voted, particularly in the South, they could not elect anyone who would oppose the Jim Crow laws.

Black civil rights organisations split

- The different black organisations split the movement towards civil rights because:
  - By mid 1920s Garvey and UNIA discredited. Garvey exposed as fraudster and he was target of FBI dirty tricks;
  - NAACP criticised by other black groups for failing to attract more black people: was dominated by white people and well-off black people;
  - Washington criticised by other black Americans for 'selling out' to whites and for accepting lower status of black Americans.

Discrimination and poverty in the north

- Most black migrants in the northern cities were more concerned with meeting their basic needs rather than participating in political action.
- Effect of migration north was to take away from the South those who had ambition and ability. Potential leaders of civil rights taken away from the South.

Black poverty in the South

- Lack of education led to inability to organise, spread information and even travel freely.
- Most sharecroppers were caught in debt traps, had limited education and were unlikely to organise themselves into campaign groups.

OVERALL

Overall, the lack of progress towards civil rights was caused by a variety of factors. Perhaps the main reason for lack of progress was institutionalised white racist attitudes in the South which showed itself in the Jim Crow laws, but the KKK was the most visible showing of the racist terror that prevented so many black Americans from campaigning for civil rights.

8. How effectively did the New Deal achieve its aims?

TOPIC AND TASK

The topic of this question is the New Deal in the 1930s in the USA.

The task of this question is to:
1. Explain what the New Deal was meant to achieve (its aims).
2. Show off detailed knowledge of what the New Deal actually achieved.
3. Reach a balanced conclusion about whether or not the New Deal achieved its aims.

STRUCTURE

Context example

In 1929 the US economy crashed. The Wall Street Crash and the depression that followed exposed the weaknesses within the US economy. The response of President Hoover and the Republican government was not enough to save them from electoral defeat in 1932. When Roosevelt became President in 1933 he promised 'a new deal for the American people'.

Introduction points to signpost:

*   What were the aims of the New Deal? Relief, Recovery and Reform.
*   The actions of the New Deal, e.g. Alphabet Agencies, action to restore confidence and stability such as bank reforms, the ending of prohibition, fireside chats.
*   Why some people criticised the New Deal.
*   The Second New Deal for the later 1930s.
*   How far the USA had recovered by the start of World War Two.

THE DEVELOPMENT SECTION

To gain K marks you must include accurate and relevant factual detail, such as:

*   Aims of the New Deal – Relief, Recovery and Reform.
*   Helping the economy: 'Alphabet Agencies', e.g. Federal Emergency Relief Administration (FERA), Tennessee Valley Authority (TVA), Public Works Administration (PWA) providing relief and work.
*   Confidence building – checking banks in 1933 to ensure they were well run and credit-worthy.
*   Repeal of prohibition.
*   Cutting wages of state employees by 15% and spending savings on relief programmes.
*   The Second New Deal 1935–1937: reforms to improve living and working conditions for many Americans.
*   Social Security Act (1935) provided a state pension scheme for the old and widows, as well as help for the disabled and poor children.
*   National Labour Relations Act (1935) gave workers the right to join trades unions.

Analysis/argument points could include:

*   Opposition from various groups, e.g. Huey Long, employers' groups formed Liberty League opposed to the New Deal.
*   Opposition to increased government intervention.
*   Roosevelt re-elected in 1936 and 1940, demonstrating his political popularity with the country at large.
*   New Deal promised more than it delivered.
*   Real economic recovery did not happen until the USA entered World War Two, with rearmament and war production.
*   On the other hand FDR's promise of 'Action and Action now!' restored confidence to a worried population who felt they were the 'forgotten men'.
*   Many of the New Deal reforms prepared the way for the longer term growth of America after the war.
*   New Deal did help America. For example the TVA brought electricity to many homes in rural areas of the South. Electricity also meant that potential new consumer goods market was expanded.
*   It gave relief, recovery and reform and these things were better than the depression years.

OVERALL

Overall, the New Deal gave hope to 'the forgotten men' in the USA of the 1930s. Although some aspects of the New Deal were more successful than others, it was in the role of restoring confidence by taking direct 'action and action now' that the New Deal met its greatest success.

9.   How far had the aims of the civil rights movement resulted in improvements in the lives of black Americans by 1968?

TOPIC AND TASK

The topic of this question is the civil rights movement in the USA in the 1950s and 1960s.

The task of this question is to:

1.   Explain what the aims of the civil rights movement were.

2.   Show knowledge of actions of the civil rights movement.

3.   Reach a balanced conclusion about the extent to which the civil rights campaigns had resulted in real improvements in the lives of black Americans by 1968.

STRUCTURE

Context example

Since the end of the civil war in the mid 19th century black Americans had faced official and legalised persecution and discrimination, especially in the South. Many black Americans moved north and west to find a better life but many just found poverty in urban ghettos. By the 1950s and 1960s black frustration boiled over and the civil rights movement gained momentum.

Introduction points to signpost:

- The aims of civil rights movement.
- Social changes by 1968, especially an end to segregation and discrimination.
- Political changes by 1968, especially voting rights.
- Economic changes by 1968, especially disadvantage in northern cities.

THE DEVELOPMENT SECTION

To gain K marks you must include accurate and relevant factual detail, such as:

Aims/social change

- An end to Jim Crow laws, segregation and obstacles to voting.
- By mid 1960s aims extended to campaigns against urban poverty.
- Campaigns such as bus boycotts, sit-ins, freedom rides, marches.
- Work of NAACP in *Brown* v. *Board of Education of Topeka*.
- Little Rock, Arkansas – desegregation of schools.
- Emergence of Martin Luther King and non-violent protest.
- Demonstrations and marches, e.g. in Birmingham, Alabama.
- March on Washington, August 1963.
- Kerner Commission 1968.

Political change

- Civil Rights Act of 1964.
- Voting restrictions in many states.
- March 1965, Selma March and media coverage of police attack on the march.
- August 1965 – the Voting Rights Act.
- 250 000 blacks newly registered by end of 1965.

Economic problems/change

- Urban problems of unemployment and bad housing.
- Urban issues more important in the north.
- Watts riots and King's failure in Chicago.
- Emergence of new leaders and ideas, such as Stokely Carmichael and Black Power, Malcolm X and Black Panthers.

Analysis/argument points could include:

Social change

- Campaigns such as bus boycotts, sit-ins, freedom rides helped demolish the Jim Crow laws.
- Work of NAACP in *Brown* v. *Board of Education of Topeka* 1954 helped to change Supreme Court decision on separate but equal.
- Desegregation of schools following national publicity at Little Rock.
- Martin Luther King and non-violent protest gained media attention and popular support for change.
- Demonstration in Birmingham, Alabama 1963 and the reaction of authorities in Birmingham, Alabama helped win over white support for change and provoked federal action.
- March on Washington, August 1963, gained massive publicity and led to the Civil Rights Act of 1964. That was a vital step to improving social conditions of black Americans.
- Negative TV coverage because of black radical campaign lost support for civil rights.
- However, Kerner Commission 1968 recognised US society still divided and change had only been limited.

Political change

- Voter registration campaigns raised public awareness of the lack of political rights for many black Americans.
- Martin Luther King believed that the Civil Rights Act of 1964 'gave Negroes some part of their rightful dignity, but without the vote it was dignity without strength'.
- March 1965, Selma March and media coverage of police attack on march gained public and political support for voting rights legislation.
- Voting Rights Act led to over 250 000 blacks newly registered by end of 1965.
- Voting Rights Act was very important step in improving political participation of black Americans.
- Vietnam War pushed civil rights campaigns from headlines. Public support declined.
- More extreme/aggressive campaigns of Black Power and Black Panthers lost public and federal authority support.

Economic change

- Urban problems of unemployment and bad housing were not helped by Civil Rights Act 1964 or voting rights.
- In the north, economic issues split the civil rights movement.
- Watts riots and King's failure in Chicago showed the weakness of old-style civil rights campaign methods.
- Emergence of new leaders and ideas, such as Stokely Carmichael and Black Power, Malcolm X and Black Panthers, increased awareness that the gains of the civil rights campaigns had been limited.

OVERALL

Overall, the achievement of the aims of the civil rights movement of the 1950s and early 1960s did lead to great changes in the lives of black Americans in the South. However, any improvement in the lives of urban blacks in the northern and western cities was more difficult to judge: it was this frustration with lack of real improvement in the ghettos of the urban centres that led to the claims that the civil rights movement had achieved only partial success by 1968.

Appeasement and the Road to War, to 1939

10. To what extent did fascist powers use tactics of threats and bullying to pursue their foreign policy aims in the years after 1933?

TOPIC AND TASK

The topic of this question is the foreign policies of Italy and Germany after 1933.

The task of this question is to:

1. Describe examples of threats and bullying used by the fascist powers in their foreign policies.
2. Explain other methods used by the fascist powers to achieve their foreign policy aims.
3. Reach a balanced conclusion that directly answers the question.

TOP EXAM TIP

If a question refers to fascist powers as this one does, do **not** refer only to Germany. You are expected to write about the foreign policies of both Germany **and** Italy.

STRUCTURE

Context example

After the 'war to end all wars' it was hoped that the League of Nations would keep the peace. However, by the 1930s Germany and Italy were prepared to use aggression to get what they wanted.

Introduction points to signpost:

* The foreign policy aims of the fascist powers.
* Growth of military force.
* Use of military force to intimidate and also to take action.
* Other methods used to achieve aims, e.g. diplomacy.

THE DEVELOPMENT SECTION

To gain K marks you must include accurate and relevant factual detail, such as:

Military force

* Fascist expansionist aims, e.g. Lebensraum, Greater Germany, Mare Nostrum.
* Fascist powers saw use of military power as legitimate tool in achieving targets.
* Military expansion and rearmament (e.g. Germany 1935).
* Examples of bullying: Italy's actions in Abyssinia, especially the use of chemical warfare.
* Evidence of fascist use of air power in Abyssinia and Spain.
* German military action in the Rhineland, Spain and threats before Anschluss and Munich.
* Threats, e.g. over Austria 1938, Polish Corridor 1939.

Other methods

* Use of diplomacy and reaching agreements:
  o German-Polish Non-Aggression Pact;
  o Stresa Front (useful to Italy for short t ime 1935–1936);
  o Anglo-German Naval Agreement;
  o Austro-German agreement;
  o Rome-Berlin Axis and Anti-Comintern Pact;
  o Munich agreement;
  o Nazi-Soviet Non-Aggression Pact.
* Nazi claims of justification, 'peaceful' intentions and 'reasonable' demands to revise Versailles, e.g. remilitarisation of the Rhineland 'justified' by France/Russia alliance.
* Careful timing and exploitation of weaknesses/divisions among potential opponents, e.g. weekend remilitarisation of the Rhineland.

Analysis/argument points could include:

Military force

The use of threats and bullying to unsettle anti-fascist powers was clear in the following actions:

* Hitler/Mussolini deliberately claimed their countries were strong countries ready to take action, thereby worrying democratic powers.
* Military expansion and rearmament (e.g. Germany 1935) alarmed and unsettled the democracies.

- Britain alarmed by Italy's ambitions in Mediterranean (Mare Nostrum) and concerned that it might lose war against Italy.
- Likewise, Italy's use of chemical warfare in Abyssinia shocked and worried European democracies. They feared that bombing would destroy civilisation. As a result, there was widespread feeling that war must be avoided at all costs.
- German military action in the Rhineland and Spain and the use of threats over Austria and the Sudetenland led to appeasement and the acceptance of German expansion in March 1938 and September 1938.
- Tactics of threats used again to prepare for action against Poland, e.g. Polish Corridor issue.

Other methods

- Agreements made between fascist powers and other European countries were always aimed at giving the fascist powers an advantage while also delaying or weakening the response of the democracies.
- Use of diplomacy to emphasise justification, 'peaceful' intentions and 'reasonable' demands to revise Versailles created reluctance to take action to prevent fascist expansion.
- Careful timing and the exploitation of weaknesses/divisions among potential opponents delayed international reaction.

OVERALL

Overall the fascist powers did use some tactics of bullying and threatening to pursue their aims but generally their tactics were more diplomatic, with implied threats rather than real ones. The fascist powers also benefited from the fears of the democracies that the fascist powers would resort to bullying and threats if they did not get their way, with the result that the fascist powers only had to hint at a threat to get their own way – until September 1939!

> 11. How far is it true to say that the policy of appeasement was a complete failure in containing the spread of fascist aggression up to March 1938?

TOPIC AND TASK

The topic of this question is the success or failure of appeasement up to March 1938.

The task of this question is to:
1. Describe the ways in which fascist aggression spread across Europe until March 1938.
2. Explain why the policy of appeasement did not contain or limit the spread of fascist aggression.
3. Consider whether appeasement did anything to limit the spread of fascist aggression in terms of the question.
4. Reach a balanced conclusion that directly answers the question.

TOP EXAM TIP

Watch out for dates in the question. The issue that is assessed by this question (issue 4) will always ask about the success of the policy of appeasement in limiting the spread of fascist aggression, between 1935 and March 1938. That means you can include Anschluss in your answer but anything about Czechoslovakia or Poland would be irrelevant and gain you no marks at all.

STRUCTURE

Context example

In the years following World War One the League of Nations represented hopes for future peace and cooperation. However, by the 1930s, Britain and France had adopted appeasement as a means of coping with fascist expansionism and aggression, but that policy seemed unable to stop Hitler from demanding more and more.

Introduction points to signpost:

- The aims of appeasement.
- German and Italian ambitions/ideology.
- Fascist aggressive actions before 1938.
- British and French reaction to fascist aggression before 1938.
- Results of British and French action.

THE DEVELOPMENT SECTION

To gain K marks you must include accurate and relevant factual detail, such as:

- Appeasement was a policy created to settle post-war grievances, reach agreement and avoid war.
- German desire for Lebensraum and Greater Germany.
- Italian desire for empire and Mare Nostrum.
- Italian invasion of Abyssinia and failure of League to take any strong action.
- Britain and France – Hoare-Laval plan.
- German rearmament.
- Anglo-German Naval Agreement.
- Stresa Front.
- Remilitarisation of the Rhineland.
- Spanish Civil War: non intervention and German/Italian involvement.
- The background to and events of Anschluss.

Analysis/argument points could include:

Abyssinia

- Examples of what action could have been taken – restrict oil supplies; block Suez Canal to **Italian** shipping. Despite strong words from Britain and France, the leaking of the Hoare-Laval plan showed that Britain and France did not intend to take strong action.

Rearmament

- Hitler was successful in reintroducing conscription and rearming and, given lack of progress with disarmament conferences, Hitler used the excuse of his enemies remaining armed to justify his rearmament.
- The Anglo-German Naval Agreement limited German naval strength to 35% of British strength, but this still allowed the German fleet to grow and signalled that Versailles prohibitions no longer applied.

Rhineland

- Hitler was successful in remilitarising the Rhineland despite his own awareness that it was a bluff.
- The remilitarisation of the Rhineland effectively closed the door on Britain and France taking any action against Germany in western Europe.
- Nazi propaganda used the remilitarisation to feed a common belief that Nazi foreign policy was only righting unfair wrongs committed by the Allies at the Versailles Treaty, thereby gaining some public support in Britain.
- By getting away with it, Hitler was encouraged to try more.

Non-intervention in Spain

- British failure to take action over German involvement in Spain also gave Hitler a signal that Britain was unable or unwilling to help democracies under threat.
- Britain's main aim was to prevent this becoming an international war, and in this was successful.
- The policy of non-intervention was supported by Britain, partly as an attempt by Britain to ensure that it would be on good terms with whoever won the war.

Anschluss

- Britain could have done little to prevent Anschluss. However, British reaction was weak and encouraged Hitler – for example, speeches by Chamberlain, public opinion that Austria was mostly German anyway and that the peace treaty that banned Anschluss was foolish. Fascist powers strengthened in the eyes of the rest of Europe. Those eyes saw Britain as weak.

OVERALL

Appeasement was in theory a policy to remove grievances, right the wrongs of the Paris peace treaties and avoid European war. From that viewpoint, appeasement was a success by March 1938. Conflicts that did occur (Abyssinia, Spain, Manchuria/China) were far away or on the edge of Europe so seemed too far away to bother about.

---

12. 'The crisis over Poland triggered World War Two.' How valid is this view?

TOPIC AND TASK

The topic of this question is the crisis over Poland and the outbreak of World War Two.

The task of this question is to:

1. Explain why there was a crisis over Poland.
2. Explain how the crisis led directly to the start of World War Two.
3. Explain other factors that could be argued as leading to World War Two.
4. Reach a balanced conclusion that directly answers the question, focussing in particular on the idea that the Polish crisis triggered the outbreak of war.

STRUCTURE

Context example

In 1919 Poland was made from land taken from Russia and Germany. Both those countries hated Poland and in 1939 both Germany and Russia tried to destroy Poland.

Introduction points to signpost:

- Nazi ambitions for Lebensraum in Russia.
- Poland next target after Hitler broke Munich agreement.
- British promise to Poland and appeasement discredited.
- British/Russian relationships in summer of 1939.
- The effect of the Nazi-Soviet agreement.
- The inevitability of war given Nazi foreign policy.

THE DEVELOPMENT SECTION

To gain K marks you must include accurate and relevant factual detail, such as:

- Munich agreement broken in March 1939.
- British and French promise to protect Romania and Poland in April 1939.

- British failure to reach agreement with Russia in summer 1939.
- Hitler's demands on Danzig and Polish Corridor.
- Hitler's long-term aims for the destruction of Versailles, including regaining of Danzig and Polish Corridor.
- Nazi-Soviet Pact August 1939.
- Events leading to Nazi invasion of Poland.

Other factors

- Hitler's long-term aims for destruction of the USSR and the winning of Russia's resources (Lebensraum).
- Hitler's need to gain new land and resources to sustain Germany's economy.
- The role of Britain's policy of appeasement in encouraging Hitler's ambitions.

Analysis/argument points could include:

- When Hitler broke the Munich agreement in March 1939 war became much more likely.
- The public realised Hitler's word was worthless and that his aims went beyond the revision of Versailles.
- Hitler's long-term aims for the destruction of Versailles, including regaining of Danzig and Polish Corridor, would result in war at some point in future.
- Those issues were triggers waiting to be pulled ever since Hitler came to power.
- Previous failures by Britain to defend its promises only encouraged Hitler to demand more.
- Hitler gambled the Polish crisis would not trigger war.
- Nazi-Soviet Pact August 1939 was vital as stepping-stone to war.
- Hitler now freed from worry of war with Russia and could use Polish Corridor crisis to provoke concessions from Poland or even a limited war.
- Britain and France very unlikely to get involved now that Russia would not be an ally.
- Hitler's miscalculation over Britain's reaction to Nazi invasion of Poland can be argued as the real cause of war.
- Given Hitler's long-term foreign policy aims and his desire to destroy the Versailles settlement, the Nazi-Soviet Pact could be seen more as a factor influencing the timing of the outbreak of war rather than as one of its underlying causes.

Other factors

- War was inevitable, given Hitler's long-term aims for destruction of the USSR and the winning of Russia's resources (Lebensraum).
- Hitler's need to gain new land and resources to sustain Germany's economy.
- Hitler's belief that British and French were 'worms' who would not turn from previous policy of appeasement and avoidance of war at all costs.
- Hitler's belief that the longer war was delayed, the more the balance of military and economic advantage would shift against Germany.

OVERALL

Overall, the Polish crisis and the German invasion of Poland was a trigger but the explosive tensions that existed had been created long before. By pulling the trigger, the tensions and worries that had been building up since the mid 1930s as a result of Nazi expansionism and the increasing inability of appeasement to control events exploded into war.

Answers to Practice Exam B, Paper 2

The Wars of Independence, 1286–1328

1. How useful is Source A as evidence of the problems caused by the death of the Maid of Norway?

   In reaching a conclusion you should refer to:
   - *the origin and possible purpose of the source;*
   - *the content of the source;*
   - *recalled knowledge.*

   5

This is a 5-mark question.

There are up to 2 marks for showing that you have <u>understood</u> the importance of the origin and the purpose of the source.

TOP EXAM TIP

You must explain why the origin and purpose make the source useful in terms of the question.

Origin:

- A letter from William Fraser requesting assistance from King Edward of England in settling the crisis caused by the death of Margaret, Maid of Norway.
- Fraser was a Guardian and Bishop of St Andrews and as such was concerned that Scotland did not fall into civil war.

Possible purpose:

- To ask Edward for help in bringing peace and stability to Scotland. Fraser is well aware of the danger of civil war if Margaret is dead.
- Fraser also wants to promote the interests of Balliol, a Comyn kinsman and clearly Fraser's preferred choice.

There are up to 2 marks for selecting three relevant parts of the source's content and:

- explaining why these selections are useful in terms of the question;
- using some recall to support and develop the points in the source.

Three relevant selections from the source are:

- … there is fear of a general war and a great slaughter of men.
- … let your Excellency approach … with an army to help save the shedding of blood and to set over Scotland a king who of right ought to have the succession …
- … speak with John Balliol so that your honour and advantage be preserved.

TOP EXAM TIP

Do **not** just list the three points from the source and leave it. You must explain why they are useful in answering the question.

Recall to support your selections could include:

- Deaths of Alexander's children and grandchildren.
- Given lack of clear succession, many feared civil war in Scotland.
- Edward feared instability on his northern border.
- Robert Bruce (the Competitor) threatened to lead an armed rising to seize power.
- Only Edward was strong enough to prevent a civil war in Scotland.
- Six Guardians appointed to manage Scotland until succession settled.
- John Balliol, Robert Bruce and John Hastings all had strong legal claims to the throne of Scotland.
- The Guardians decided to ask Edward to make a choice.

There are up to 2 marks for using relevant and accurate recall that shows a wider knowledge of the issues and links to the question, such as:

- Edward pressured the Competitors to agree to his overlordship.
- The Treaty of Birgham had established a secure future with England by arranged marriage between Margaret and Edward's son.
- Edward's ambitions towards Scotland – attempts to establish overlordship.
- Bishop of Durham to help administer in Scotland.
- Edward brought his army to Norham. His navy prepared to blockade Scotland.
- Edward raised new taxes to prepare for a possible war against Scotland.
- Edward's lawyers argued that it was up to the Guardians to prove that he was not overlord.
- Edward argued that English kings had a legal claim to the overlordship of Scotland.
- King Edward gained recognition of his overlordship from the claimants.
- John Balliol was forced to accept that he was a vassal of the English king.

TOP EXAM TIP

Never just include information because you think it is about the topic of the question. You must always link it to answering the question by writing something like: 'This information helps to explain the usefulness of the source because …'

---

2.   How fully does Source B show the changing relationship between John Balliol and Edward I?
      Use the source and recalled knowledge.
                                                                                          10

This is a 10-mark question.
There are up to 4 marks for selecting four relevant parts of the source's content and:

- explaining why these selections are relevant in terms of the question;
- using some recall to support and develop the points in the source.

Four relevant selections from the source are:

- John was ordered to appear to fight for Edward, in much the same way as the great earls of England were.
- The assumption that the Scots were to fight against France, Scotland's largest trading partner, was worse.
- The demands for taxes from the Scottish nobility to fund and prepare for the war.
- In 1295 six new Guardians were appointed by the Community of the Realm to defy King Edward. They sent envoys to the King of France and at the beginning of 1296 a treaty against Edward was agreed.

TOP EXAM TIP

Do **not** just list the four points from the source and leave it. You must explain why they are helpful in answering the question.

Recall to support your selections could include:

- King John had made a voluntary promise to pay homage to Edward in front of witnesses.
- John Balliol recognised Edward I as his superior lord. That meant that Balliol had to serve Edward. If Balliol broke his promise Edward could claim back his lands.
- Edward demanded feudal military forces from Scotland to go to war against Philip IV of France in 1294.
- The Treaty of Birgham had asserted Scotland's independence as a nation – 'the rights, laws, liberties and customs of the kingdom of Scotland shall be wholly and completely preserved for all time throughout the whole Scotland'.
- January 1293, John was forced to release Edward from any promises made at the Treaty of Birgham.
- All of Edward's promises at Norham were to be ignored.
- Edward had demonstrated his superiority by ordering John to attend his parliament and also by overruling decisions made by King John.
- Wool trade with France and Flanders was vital to Scottish economy. War between England and France made trade difficult but if Scotland had to fight against France the trade would stop entirely.
- The Guardians signed a treaty with France in John's name – historians argue whether Balliol had been sidelined or not. Was Balliol asserting his independence of action, taking a stand against Edward or did significant nobles in Scotland (the Community of the Realm) realise that Balliol could not defend Scottish interests and so took action on their own?

TOP EXAM TIP

Use the word **partly**! By saying you agree _partly_, or a source explains something _partly_, you have the opportunity to explain what the points made in the source mean. You can then write something like, 'On the other hand' and then bring in lots of recall to suggest things that are relevant to the question but were not mentioned in the source. By doing this you will be able to demonstrate your own recalled knowledge and you will also have a balanced answer that answers a 'How fully?' question.

There are up to 7 marks for using relevant and accurate recall that shows a wider knowledge of the issues and links to the question, such as:

- John was forced to swear fealty to Edward for all his lands, not just his lands in England.
- Edward had the wording of the royal seal of Scotland changed.
- Edward forced John to accept Edward's appointments as major players in Scotland's administration, e.g. Master Thomas of Hunsingore to be his new chancellor.
- Edward had used legal cases to assert his superiority over Balliol.
- Edward allowed the wine merchant Macduff to appeal to the English court over the head of King John.
- Edward refused to acknowledge King John's representative and demanded Balliol attend in person.
- After Edward's invasion of Scotland in 1296 and the defeat of the Scots at Dunbar, Balliol was forced to surrender his throne.
- Balliol was stripped of his royal insignia and taken to London as prisoner.

---

3. To what extent do Sources C and D agree about the reasons for defeat at Falkirk and continuing Scottish resistance?

   Compare the sources overall and in detail.

   5

The comparison question is worth 5 marks.

You must start your answer by making an OVERALL COMPARISON. There are up to 2 marks for making an overall comparison. An overall comparison of the sources should include:

- Overall, the sources disagree over Wallace's responsibility for defeat and the end of his role as Guardian of Scotland. The sources disagree over the reasons for defeat at Falkirk and the consequences of that defeat for Wallace.

• Source C argues that Wallace must take responsibility for the defeat and afterwards he had little credibility as a leader of resistance against England. On the other hand, Source D believes that Wallace was betrayed and disillusioned but kept up a brave resistance against England.

You must continue your answer by comparing the sources IN DETAIL.

There are up to 4 marks for finding four different sets of comparison points within the sources.

> **TOP EXAM TIP**
>
> It is not enough just to quote a sentence from one source, then compare by quoting from another. You must also explain the point being made by your extracts in your own words and use some recall to develop your comparison. That is what is meant by a developed comparison.

In detail:

1. The sources disagree over Wallace's responsibility for defeat.
    • Source C thinks that 'Wallace should have avoided battle against the superior English forces but he had seriously misjudged them.'
    • On the other hand, Source D believes 'The victory of Falkirk was granted to the enemy through the treachery of the Scots nobles.'
2. The sources disagree over the role of the Comyns in the defeat.
    • Source C states 'Later historians said that Wallace had been deliberately abandoned by Scots noblemen including the Comyns who deserted the battlefield. However, in reality the Scottish nobility on horseback were simply outnumbered by the English cavalry.'
    • On the other hand, Source D blames 'the obvious wickedness of the Comyns'.
3. The sources disagree over the way in which Wallace ceased being Guardian of Scotland.
    • Source C states that after the battle of Falkirk, 'Wallace's defeat at Falkirk ruined his image of invincibility. Wallace was forced to resign his title as Guardian of Scotland'
    • On the other hand, Source D believes that Wallace gave up being Guardian 'of his own accord'.
4. The sources disagree over the settlement reached with Edward in 1304.
    • Source C suggests that Scotland surrendered completely in 1304 by stating 'in 1304 the Scots leaders ... surrendered and recognised Edward as their overlord'
    • On the other hand, Source D suggests there was continued resistance against England by writing 'Wallace kept alive the hopes of his countrymen and bravely resisted the English when other cowards in Scotland knelt in surrender to the English invaders.'

In conclusion, Source C takes the view that Wallace made mistakes and had outlived his usefulness after the defeat at Falkirk whereas Source D keeps alive the image of Wallace as betrayed and undefeated in his resistance to England and his struggle for a free Scotland.

> **TOP EXAM TIP**
>
> You do not have to end with a short conclusion that directly answers the question asked, but it can help!

> **4.** How far does Source E illustrate the reasons for Bruce's victory over his Scottish opponents?
> *Use the source and recalled knowledge.*
>
> **10**

This is a 10-mark question.

There are up to 4 marks for selecting four relevant parts of the source's content and:
• explaining why these selections are relevant in terms of the question;
• using some recall to support and develop the points in the source.

Four relevant selections from the source are:
• Having put all his enemies to flight at every place he came to and having taken their fortresses and levelled them to the ground ...
• He destroyed the walls and ditches and consumed everything else with fire.
• On January 8, the town of Perth was taken ... and the disloyal people both English and Scots were taken, dragged and slain with the sword.
• The king in his clemency spared the rabble and granted forgiveness to those that asked it.

> **TOP EXAM TIP**
>
> Do **not** just list the four points from the source and leave it. You must explain why they are helpful in answering the question.

Recall to support your selections could include:

• Edward Bruce defeated Donald of the Isles in Galloway.
• Bruce subdued Argyll and besieged Dunstaffnage Castle.
• Edward Bruce subdued Galloway with great violence.
• The subjugation of Argyll was part of Bruce's more general campaign to exert royal authority in the west.
• Bruce besieged a number of castles (e.g. Urquhart) as part of his campaign against his Scottish rivals. Other castles were captured by trickery, e.g. Linlithgow, Roxburgh, Edinburgh.
• Destruction of enemy castles to prevent them being reoccupied and saving Bruce the expense of garrisons.
• Those who still resisted Bruce were shown no mercy, as a warning to others, e.g. Herschip of Buchan.
• Bruce often treated defeated enemies with some leniency, offering safe passage to England.
• Many former enemies eventually became allies, such as the Earl of Ross.

There are up to 7 marks for using relevant and accurate recall that shows a wider knowledge of the issues and links to the question, such as:

• Bruce won the civil war for a variety of reasons:
   ○ Comyns were weakened by the murder of John Comyn;
   ○ Bruce quickly attracted a following which gave him a reputation for invincibility.
• 'Bruce myth' which demoralised his opponents.
• He attacked Buchan from the north, where it was weakly defended.
• His use of mercenary fighters gathered in the west of Scotland.
• He gave his campaign legitimacy by his coronation, which was supported by some leading churchmen and members of the Community of the Realm.
• Bruce was lucky not to face opposition from the English during the period of the civil war.

Migration and Empire, 1830–1939

1. How useful is Source A as evidence of the push and pull factors influencing emigration from Scotland?

    In reaching a conclusion you should refer to:
    • *the origin and possible purpose of the source;*
    • *the content of the source;*
    • *recalled knowledge.*   5

This is a 5-mark question.

There are up to 2 marks for showing that you have <u>understood</u> the importance of the origin and the purpose of the source.

> **TOP EXAM TIP**
> You must explain why the origin and purpose make the source useful in terms of the question.

Origin:

• Canadian Emigration Office poster from the early twentieth century when Canada wanted to encourage emigration to open up its interior territory.

Possible purpose:

• To persuade people to emigrate to Canada. It is designed to give positive 'pull' reasons for emigrants to come to Canada and certainly gives no indication of any difficulties emigrants might face.

There are up to 2 marks for selecting three relevant parts of the source's content and:

• explaining why these selections are useful in terms of the question;
• using some recall to support and develop the points in the source.

Three relevant selections from the source are:

• Image shows positive attraction of land, transport and bright future, confirmed by many people in a crowd heading westwards to new lands.
• Health concerns were a major issue in Scotland. By showing the word 'Health' prominently, the poster implies Canada is a much healthier place than Scotland.
• Poverty was a big problem in Scotland, along with land shortage. The poster appeals to both concerns by showing a healthy, cheerful person, implying wealth will be available as will land 'for the asking'.

> **TOP EXAM TIP**
> Do **not** just list the three points from the source and leave it. You must explain why they are helpful in answering the question.

Recall to support your selections could include:

- Land issue in Highlands.
- Dispossessed farmers from lowland Scotland.
- Canadian emigration officers were very active in Scotland. Offices in Glasgow and Inverness.
- Travelling reps promoting Canadian emigration operating in Scotland, some speaking Gaelic.
- Availability of cheap land in the Empire, especially Canada.
- Information about successes of Scots emigrants in Canada, Australia and New Zealand.
- The Empire Settlement Act 1922 – efforts to increase emigration from Britain to Canada and other countries in the Empire. The legislation was the basis for all of the settlement schemes developed in the 1920s, including the '3000 British Families' settlement scheme, and the emigration of domestic servants, juveniles and farm workers.
- Easy access to Canadian interior after opening of Canadian Pacific Railway (railway shown in poster, middle distance).

There are up to 2 marks for using relevant and accurate recall that shows a wider knowledge of the issues and links to the question, such as:

- Scots prominent in opening up the wilds of Canada – Scots discovered and named many rivers and mountains, and created new settlements.
- In Canada, Scots dominated government, fur trade, education and banking.
- Many Scots became governors of Canada.
- George Stephen organising finance and creation of Canadian Pacific Railroad.
- Sir John A. MacDonald, first Prime Minister of Canada when it became a Dominion.
- Religious development through Church of Scotland.
- Contribution to laws and learning/education (e.g. McGill University).
- Push reasons for emigration such as:
  - Effects of Highland Clearances;
  - Industrialisation – decline in craftwork, e.g. handloom weavers;
  - Problems in fishing industry;
  - Decline of Highland industries, e.g. kelp manufacture;
  - Slum conditions in the cities;
  - Disease, particularly cholera in the cities;
  - Periodic unemployment resulting from the trade cycle.

TOP EXAM TIP

Never just include information because you think it is about the topic of the question. You must always link it to answering the question by writing something like: 'This information helps to explain the usefulness of the source because ...'

---

2. How fully does Source B illustrate the experience of immigrants in Scotland?

   Use the source and recalled knowledge.

   10

This is a 10-mark question.

There are up to 4 marks for selecting four relevant parts of the source's content and:

- explaining why these selections are relevant in terms of the question;
- using some recall to support and develop the points in the source.

Four relevant selections from the source are:

- Lithuanians were seen as competition in the market for jobs.
- Employers were often accused of using Lithuanians as strike breakers.
- Lithuanians were devoutly Catholic in a fiercely Presbyterian land.
- Trades unions were openly hostile, claiming that the newcomers' lack of English made them a danger at work.

TOP EXAM TIP

Do **not** just list the four points from the source and leave it. You must explain why they are useful in answering the question.

Recall to support your selections could include:

- Lithuanians arrived in much fewer numbers than Irish immigrants and, mostly, were not thought of as a threat to Scottish way of life by native Scots.
- Lithuanians often worked in mining areas of West Lothian.
- In small communities newcomers seen as unwelcome competition for jobs.

- Newcomers seen as a threat to wage stability as employers could offer lower wages on take it or leave it basis; the Glasgow Trades Council declared the Lithuanians in Glengarnock as 'an evil'.
- Newcomers seen as a means of employers challenging power of trades unions and weakening the strike weapon used to improve conditions and wages.
- Scottish Protestants already wary of Catholic Irish workers now saw another group of Catholics within their communities.
- On other hand, Lithuanians changed their names to ease assimilation.
- Lithuanians were generally fewer in numbers and in some areas assimilated well.

> **TOP EXAM TIP**
>
> Use the word **partly!** By saying you agree partly, or a source explains something partly, you have the opportunity to explain what the points made in the source mean. You can then write something like, 'On the other hand' and then bring in lots of recall to suggest things that are relevant to the question but were not mentioned in the source. By doing this you will be able to demonstrate your own recalled knowledge and you will also have a balanced answer that answers a 'How fully?' question.

There are up to 7 marks for using relevant and accurate recall that shows a wider knowledge of the issues and links to the question, such as:

- Other immigrant groups to Scotland included Jews and Italians. All experienced similar problems to a greater or lesser degree.
- Each immigrant group formed self-contained settlements partly for comfort and partly from difficulty in assimilation.
- To an extent these groups experienced similar linguistic and religious difficulties.
- The numbers of these immigrant groups were significantly lower than Irish immigrants and so perhaps were perceived as less of a threat to Scottish society.
- Jews began to arrive after WW1 in smaller numbers than Irish immigrants and assimilated more easily into Scottish society.
- Italians were accepted into Scottish society fairly readily.
- Some opposition to ice cream parlours as places of trouble and decadence.
- Most Italians did not aim at assimilation but intended to return to 'old country' having made money.
- These groups, perhaps, were more willing to assimilate than Irish immigrants.
- Irish immigrants did assimilate as time passed – trade union membership, intermarriage with Scots, political involvement and fighting in British army against Germany during the Great War.
- Upon arrival, immigrants in general lived in poorest areas of towns, where they were subject to the same slum conditions and the ravages of disease experienced by native Scots who remained.
- Immigrants often highly motivated to improve their lives by working long hours.
- Many immigrant groups were able to move to better-off areas as they became wealthier.
- Local groups often expressed jealousies against socially mobile immigrant groups.
- Irish Catholics set up own churches, schools and organisations. On other hand, often seen as drunken and superstitious.
- Role of Irish immigrants in developing Scottish roads, railways, canals, industry, agriculture.
- More accepting and positive attitude towards Protestant Irish.

3. To what extent do Sources C and D disagree about the impact of Scots emigrants on the growth and development of the Empire?

   Compare the sources overall and in detail.   5

The comparison question is worth 5 marks.

You must start your answer by making an OVERALL COMPARISON. There are up to 2 marks for making an overall comparison. An overall comparison of the sources should include:

- Overall the sources disagree about the impact of Scots on the growth and development of the Empire.
- Source C argues that Scots have little to offer the colony and in fact even damage the colony, whereas Source D argues that Scots have been very important to the development of colonies within the Empire.

You must continue your answer by comparing the sources IN DETAIL.

There are up to 4 marks for finding four different sets of comparison points within the sources.

> **TOP EXAM TIP**
>
> It is not enough just to quote a sentence from one source, then compare by quoting from another. You must also explain the point being made by your extracts in your own words and use some recall to develop your comparison. That is what is meant by a developed comparison.

In detail:

1. The sources disagree about the literacy and education of Scots colonists.
   - Source C claims that Scots cannot get employment because they are uneducated and states 'Their total ignorance of the English language makes it difficult to get employment for them'.
   - On the other hand, Source D states 'most Scots could read and write, and spoke English'.

2. The sources disagree about the contribution of Scots to the development of the Empire.
   - Source C claims that Scots made no worthwhile contribution and states 'their laziness and extremely filthy habits have not made a good impression on the British people already here'.
   - On the other hand, Source D argues that Scots had a good reputation and did help to develop the Empire, stating 'Far from being "lazy" and ignorant ... Scots had a reputation as good workers'.

3. The sources disagree about the contribution to the development and civilisation of the Empire.
   - Source C thinks Scots are damaging the development of the Empire and states 'it cannot be argued other than their arrival is having a most unwelcome and detrimental effect on the inhabitants of this colony'.
   - On the other hand, Source D thinks Scots are helping to develop and 'civilise' the Empire and claims 'most Scots made a vital contribution to the development of the Empire ... Scots missionaries brought to societies the word of God to "dark continents" around the world'.

4. The sources disagree about the wider contribution of Scots to the development of the Empire in terms of what they could offer.
   - Source C argues that 'these wretches have little to offer this society' and that the migration of Scots should be limited – 'It would be better if such immigration was restricted'.
   - On the other hand, Source D argues that 'Scottish soldiers and explorers opened up the new colonies' and that more Scots are wanted, since 'Scots who were doctors, lawyers, engineers, accountants or architects were also in high demand'.

In conclusion, while Source C has a very negative view of Scots and their contribution to the Empire, Source D believes Scots and their energies and skills have helped to civilise and develop the Empire in many different ways.

TOP EXAM TIP

You do not have to end with a short conclusion that directly answers the question asked, but it will impress the examiner!

---

4. How far does Source E illustrate the contribution of immigrants to Scottish society and culture?
   Use the source and recalled knowledge.
   10

This is a 10-mark question.

There are up to 4 marks for selecting four relevant parts of the source's content and:

- explaining why these selections are relevant in terms of the question;
- using some recall to support and develop the points in the source.

Four relevant selections from the source are:

- The Italians in Scotland quickly became committed to the catering trade.
- New consumer delights for the working class – fish suppers and ice cream.
- The Italian community attracted less hostility because they posed little threat to native workers or wages.
- At first the Italian immigrants made few social contacts with the rest of Scottish society. For many the hope was to return to Italy, so assimilation seemed pointless.

TOP EXAM TIP

Do **not** just list the four points from the source and leave it. You must explain why they are helpful in answering the question.

Recall to support your selections could include:

- Number of Italian cafés/takeaways in Glasgow: 1903 – 89; 1905 – 337.
- By the 1920s, the barrows of 'the Hokey Pokey men' had grown into luxury ice cream parlours in the city centres, e.g. Nardini's, with art deco furnishings and first ever soda fountain in the UK. Largest café in Britain.
- By the 1930s, many Italian family firms were well established in Scotland. Local examples: Valvona & Crolla in Edinburgh 1934, Luca's in Musselburgh, Giaccopazzi in Eyemouth.
- Some tension between Catholic Italians and Presbyterian Scots. Many Scottish Presbyterian Church leaders were unhappy that Italian cafés opened on the Sabbath.
- The cafés were sometimes the scene of unruly behaviour. A *Glasgow Herald* article claimed ice cream parlours were morally corrupt and reported the 'ice cream hell'.
- There was a greater degree of acceptance from the temperance movement as the cafés chose not to sell alcohol.
- As businesses grew, family members from Italy came to join their relatives in Scotland.

- The owners and employees of cafés often worked 14-hour days, seven days a week. Employees were usually family members.

There are up to 7 marks for using relevant and accurate recall that shows a wider knowledge of the issues and links to the question, such as:

- In 1861 there were about 120 Italians in Scotland, the majority of them in Glasgow. By 1901 the Italian population was 4051.
- At first many Italian immigrants made a living by becoming peddlers, selling religious craft items door to door, such as plaster statues.
- Glasgow had the third largest Italian community in the United Kingdom.
- Italians initially established themselves in areas of Glasgow, such as Partick and Garnethill in the West End of Glasgow.
- Apart from catering trades, Italians were also found as craftsmen, entertainers, itinerant traders and peddlers, organ grinders (street entertainment) and plaster figure makers.
- In addition to catering, Italians became established as hairdressers – they set up the College of Italian Hairdressers in Glasgow in 1928.
- Children of immigrants were expected to marry into other Italian families. This led to the community being seen as insular and unwilling to mix with the wider society.

Scotland and the Impact of the Great War, 1914–1928

1. How useful is Source A as evidence of why so many young Scots joined the army in 1914?

   In reaching a conclusion you should refer to:
   - *the origin and possible purpose of the source;*
   - *the content of the source;*
   - *recalled knowledge.*

   5

This is a 5-mark question.

There are up to 2 marks for showing that you have <u>understood</u> the importance of the origin and the purpose of the source.

> **TOP EXAM TIP**
> You must explain why the origin and purpose make the source useful in terms of the question.

Origin:

- A British recruitment poster from 1914. War had broken out and the British army had very few soldiers. The government decided to launch a poster campaign to encourage young men to join up.

Possible purpose:

- This poster is meant to appeal to young Scots. Posters such as this were used to persuade young men to join the army at a time when there was no conscription and all enlistment was voluntary in the UK.

There are up to 2 marks for selecting three relevant parts of the source's content and:

- explaining why these selections are useful in terms of the question;
- using some recall to support and develop the points in the source.

Three relevant selections from the source are:

- An appeal to patriotism – your king and country need you.
- An appeal to Scots – the poster shows a 'kiltie' soldier standing guard in France or Belgium (French street-sign on wall).
- An appeal to honour – to protect the Empire and also to keep the promise made in the 'scrap of paper' to protect Belgium.

> **TOP EXAM TIP**
> Do **not** just list the three points from the source and leave it. You must explain why they are useful in answering the question.

Recall to support your selections could include:

- Regular army, called British Expeditionary Force (BEF), sent to France within days of war starting.
- In August 1914 BEF only numbered 180 000, most of whom were in India at outbreak.
- Kitchener's appeal for thousands of young men easily passed by rush to volunteer.
- Kitchener General Secretary for War. Leete's poster showing Kitchener was most famous using the words 'your king and country need you'.

- Poster appealed to Scots martial traditions.
- Image of kiltie soldier a powerful one in early 20th century Scotland.
- By the end of the first week in September 1914, Glasgow had recruited more than 22 000 men.
- By December 1914, 25% of the male labour force of western Scotland had already joined the army. Scottish 'pals' battalions – such as Cranston's, McCrae's, the Tramways and the Boys' Brigade.
- Highland regiments had played big part in building British Empire and were portrayed in comics and books as heroes.

> **TOP EXAM TIP**
>
> Never just include information because you think it is about the topic of the question. You must always link it to answering the question by writing something like: 'This information helps to explain the usefulness of the source because ...'

There are up to 2 marks for using relevant and accurate recall that shows a wider knowledge of the issues and links to the question, such as:

- British army in August 1914 small in comparison to German army.
- Scrap of paper was Kaiser's reference to Treaty of London 1839 that guaranteed Belgian neutrality.
- Belgium attacked as part of German Schlieffen plan.
- No conscription in Britain until 1916.
- Other methods of persuading men to join up included:
    - Appeals to guilt – Daddy what did you do in the war?
    - Appeals to dislike of Germans. 'He (the Kaiser) won't be happy until he gets it (Europe).'
- Other influences on joining up – helping mates, helping countrymen in danger, avoiding female disapproval, escaping boring jobs, escaping unemployment, desire for excitement and adventure, get involved before the excitement is 'over by Christmas'.
- Huge sacrifice of Scots during the war – one in five British casualties was Scottish.

> 2. How fully does Source B illustrate the impact of the war on Scottish society?
>
> *Use the source and recalled knowledge.*
>
> 10

This is a 10-mark question.

There are up to 4 marks for selecting four relevant parts of the source's content and:

- explaining why these selections are useful in terms of the question;
- using some recall to support and develop the points in the source.

Four relevant selections from the source are:

- I married during the war, in 1917. I married a man who was gassed and came back from the war.
- I went into a single room apartment in Govan and then got a job at an engineering works.
- During the war years there were people getting put out of their homes because they couldn't pay the rent. Earlier there was the Rent Strike ... But then the Rent Restriction Act was brought in and made it easier.
- I think it was due to the work of Baillie Mary Barbour particularly and the women that the Rent Restriction Act was brought into being.

> **TOP EXAM TIP**
>
> Do **not** just list the four points from the source and leave it. You must explain why they are useful to answering the question.

Recall to support your selections could include:

- Huge sacrifice of Scots during the war – of 557 000 Scots who enlisted in the services, 26·4% lost their lives. One in five British casualties was Scottish.
- Many casualties were 'unseen' – now called post-traumatic stress disorder.
- High numbers of unmarried women in post-war Scotland as result of high casualties. Impact on birth rate. Was there a lost generation of talent?
- In 1911, 6000 women were employed in the heavy industries of Clydeside; by the end of the war 31 500 women were working in the munitions industry.
- The war allowed women, temporarily, to step into jobs vacated by male workers serving in the armed forces or to be employed in heavy industries under the dilution scheme.
- Rent strikes in Glasgow, Dundee, Aberdeen and elsewhere.
- Tensions in housing market brought about by wartime conditions.
- Landlords seen as unfair and exploitative when men away fighting.
- They would argue rising rent was effect of supply and demand.
- Resistance to evictions.
- Sympathy strikes in engineering works and shipyards.

- Rent Restriction Act brought state intervention in the private housing rental market for the first time.
- Prominent role played by women like Mary Barbour, Helen Crawfurd and Agnes Dollan.
- Women taking role in local politics.
- Women more active in roles in ILP and Labour Party.

TOP EXAM TIP

Use the word **partly!** By saying you agree <u>partly</u>, or a source explains something <u>partly</u>, you have the opportunity to explain what the points made in the source mean. You can then write something like, 'On the other hand' and then bring in lots of recall to suggest things that are relevant to the question but were not mentioned in the source. By doing this you will be able to demonstrate your own recalled knowledge and you will also have a balanced answer that answers a 'How fully?' question.

There are up to 7 marks for using relevant and accurate recall that shows a wider knowledge of the issues and links to the question, such as:

- Disproportionate effect of losses in rural Scotland in particular.
- Disproportionate losses of officers had an impact on leadership in Scotland and a knock-on effect on industry after the war.
- Women were already important in some industries before the war, e.g. textile trade, domestic service, farming and jute industry in Dundee.
- The average pay for women was 45% of what was paid to men.
- Women worked in many other industries during the war including the railways and rubber industries.
- The number of women working increased from 593 210 in 1911 to 638 575 a decade later.
- In the course of the war, the National Federation of Women Workers increased its membership from 10 000 to 50 000.
- Many of the gains made by women during the war were lost when soldiers returned from France expecting their jobs back.
- Representation of the People Act gave women the vote in national elections for the first time.

---

3. To what extent do Sources C and D agree about the effects of rationing on Scottish society during the war?
   Compare the sources overall and in detail. **5**

The comparison question is worth 5 marks.

You must start your answer by making an OVERALL COMPARISON. There are up to 2 marks for making an overall comparison. An overall comparison of the sources should include:

- Overall the sources disagree about the effect of rationing on Scottish society during the war.
- Source C argues that rationing had serious effects on Scottish society with people telling the writer 'how bad it had been'. On the other hand, Source D suggests that rationing did not cause serious problems and, in fact, the system worked well.

You must continue your answer by comparing the sources IN DETAIL.

There are up to 4 marks for finding four different sets of comparison points within the sources.

TOP EXAM TIP

It is not enough just to quote a sentence from one source, then compare by quoting from another. You must also explain the point being made by your extracts in your own words and use some recall to develop your comparison. That is what is meant by a developed comparison.

In detail:

1. The sources disagree about the level of hunger suffered by the population.
   - Source C claims the food shortages led to serious problems – 'Many, especially children, died of starvation.'
   - On the other hand, Source D states 'we were never faced with famine or actual privation'. It's possible that Young in Source C is exaggerating since he only heard those stories when he came back after the war. On the other hand, Lloyd George was Prime Minister so he would make the system sound as if it all worked well.
2. The sources disagree about how serious the food shortages were.
   - Source C claims his family only lived on 'bones from the butcher made into soups. And stale bread.'
   - On the other hand, Source D states 'compulsory temperance in eating was in general more beneficial than harmful in its effects'. Rationing was an attempt to make sure people got fair shares. As food supplies became scarcer, prices started to rise. Food rationing stopped some people having too much food but made sure everyone had enough.
3. The sources disagree about the efficiency of the food supply during the rationing years.
   - Source C says 'When some food did get delivered to the shops everyone for miles around crowded round the place. The queues stretched for miles.'

- On the other hand, Source D says 'this rationing system ensured a regular ... food supply'. Photographs of the time do show long queues but some rationed food was scarcer so people had to queue when supplies did eventually arrive.

4. The sources disagree over the how people reacted to the food shortages.
    - Source C claims 'Food riots were very common' and, 'if you were old or unsteady on your feet you stood no chance', suggesting there were struggles to grab enough food.
    - On the other hand, Source D says 'Credit is due to our people for the loyal manner in which they submitted themselves to these ... restrictions. Without general goodwill it would have been impossible to make the regulations effective.'

In conclusion, while Source C reports that food shortages caused many problems, Source D suggests that rationing was a good and fair response to the wartime disruption to the food supply.

TOP EXAM TIP

You do not have to end with a short conclusion that directly answers the question asked, but it can help!

---

4. How far does Source E show the impact of the war on the growth of radicalism, the ILP and Red Clydeside?

    Use the source and recalled knowledge.　　　　　　　　　　　　　　　　　　　　　　**10**

This is a 10-mark question.

There are up to 4 marks for selecting four relevant parts of the source's content and:

- explaining why these selections are useful in terms of the question;
- using some recall to support and develop the points in the source.

Four relevant selections from the source are:

- Glasgow during the First World War gained the reputation of being a centre of socialist if not communist ideas, a hotbed of revolution.
- Protest against 'dilution'.
- Some of the socialist leaders, including John Maclean, opposed the war; others, including David Kirkwood, did not.
- In the 1922 General Election ten Labour MPs were elected for Glasgow constituencies.

TOP EXAM TIP

Do **not** just list the four points from the source and leave it. You must explain why they are useful in answering the question.

Recall to support your selections could include:

- Willie Gallacher: prominent militant trade unionist, founding member of the Communist Party in 1920. Gallacher was consistently anti-war, but socialists were split on the matter.
- John Maclean won the support of thousands of people with his socialist and anti-war views.
- Origin of much radicalism from the shop stewards on Clyde – numerous strikes on the Clyde.
- More evidence of radical opinions seen in the growth of the Labour Party.
- Radicalism after war: possible 'revolution' in 1919 – George Square; but long-term triumph of gradualist approach represented by Maxton, Kirkwood, Johnston, Wheatley, as opposed to Maclean who wanted revolution.

There are up to 7 marks for using relevant and accurate recall that shows a wider knowledge of the issues and links to the question, such as:

- In the 1922 election Labour made the breakthrough as the second political party: 29 of their 142 seats were in Scotland; 10 of these were in Glasgow.
- More radical nature of Glasgow's Labour MPs can be seen in the fact that they were members of the ILP, which had a more socialist agenda than the Labour Party.
- In the 1922 General Election in Scotland, 40 out of the total of 43 prospective Labour candidates were members of the ILP.
- Labour support increased ten times between 1910 and 1918.
- In 1922, 42% of Glasgow electors voted for Labour.
- Labour won 10 out of 15 seats (previously only held one).
- In 1922, Labour won 29 seats in Scotland (10 in Glasgow) and then in 1924 they won 34 seats.
- Membership of the Independent Labour Party trebled during the war years.
- Radical leaders like John Maclean, Willie Gallacher, Jimmy Maxton and John Muir emerged during the war.
- Clydeside was the main centre of communist politics after formation of British Communist Party in 1920.